P9-DDI-141

EARTH'S CYCLES

TEAM GREEN SCIENCE PROJECTS

GREEN SCIENCE PROJECTS ABOUT THE WATER CYCLE, PHOTOSYNTHESIS, AND MORE

Robert Gardner

Enslow Publishers, Inc.
40 Industrial Road
Box 398
Berkeley Heights, NJ 07922
USA
http://www.enslow.com

EARTH'S CYCLES

GREEN Science Projects About the Water Cycle, Photosynthesis, and More

Library of Congress Cataloging-in-Publication Data

Gardner, Robert, 1929–
Earth's cycles : green science projects about the water cycle, photosynthesis, and more / by Robert Gardner.
p. cm. — (Team Green science projects)
Includes bibliographical references and index.
ISBN 978-0-7660-3644-4
1. Hydrologic cycle—Juvenile literature. 2. Solar cycle—Juvenile literature. 3. Biogeochemical cycle—Juvenile literature. 4. Greenhouse gases—Juvenile literature. I. Title.
GB848.G37 2011
577'.14—dc22

2010025816

Printed in the United States of America

112010 Lake Book Manufacturing, Inc., Melrose Park, IL

10 9 8 7 6 5 4 3 2 1

To Our Readers: We have done our best to make sure all Internet Addresses in this book were active and appropriate when we went to press. However, the author and the publisher have no control over and assume no liability for the material available on those Internet sites or on other Web sites they may link to. Any comments or suggestions can be sent by e-mail to comments@enslow.com or to the address on the back cover.

♻ Enslow Publishers, Inc., is committed to printing our books on recycled paper. The paper in every book contains 10% to 30% post-consumer waste (PCW). The cover board on the outside of each book contains 100% PCW. Our goal is to do our part to help young people and the environment too!

Illustration Credits: Jonathan Moreno, pp. 20, 24, 27, 65; Stephen F. Delisle, pp. 38, 47, 69, 85; Stephen Rountree (www.rountreegraphics.com), pp. 16, 17, 31 (light), 49, 61, 72, 74, 90, 92, 93, 99; Tom LaBaff and Stephanie LaBaff, 31, 35, 82.

Photo Credits: © beyond fotomedia/Photolibrary, p. 1; © Inga Spence/Photo Researchers, Inc., p. 84; Shutterstock.com, pp. 6, 8, 11, 13, 25, 58, 63, 70.

Cover Photo: © beyond fotomedia/Photolibrary

Contents

Introduction 5

Chapter 1

The Solar Cycle: Sustaining All Other Cycles 12

- ✓ 1.1 Directions from a Shadow Cast by the Midday Sun: A Measurement 14
- ✓ 1.2 Checking Your North-South Line: A Measurement 19
- 1.3 Find Two Cycles of the Sun by Watching Sunrise and Sunset: Observations 22
- 1.4 Mapping the Sun's Path Across the Sky: An Experiment 26
- ✓ 1.5 How Earth Creates the Apparent Cycles of the Sun: Models 29
- ✓ 1.6 Season Cycles and the Sun: Models 34

Chapter 2

The Carbon and Oxygen Cycles 37

- 2.1 Decomposition and Carbon: A Demonstration 43
- 2.2 Starch: A Test 45
- 2.3 Photosynthesis, Leaves, and Stored Food: An Experiment 46
- 2.4 Photosynthesis and Carbon Dioxide: An Author Experiment 47
- 2.5 Photosynthesis and Carbon Dioxide: A Demonstration 50
- ✓ 2.6 Photosynthesis and Grass in Light and Darkness: An Experiment 52
- 2.7 How Plants Adapt to Receive Maximum Light: An Experiment 53

✓ Indicates experiments that offer ideas for science fair projects.

Chapter 3

Carbon Dioxide: The Most Abundant Greenhouse Gas 55

3.1 Carbon Dioxide: A Chemical Test 56
3.2 Two Properties of Carbon Dioxide: An Experiment ... 57
3.3 Air, Lung-Air, and Carbon Dioxide: An Experiment ... 59
3.4 Preparation and Density of Carbon Dioxide: A Measurement 64

Chapter 4

The Water, Nitrogen, and Phosphorus Cycles 68

4.1 The Water Cycle: A Model 71
4.2 Evaporation of Ocean Water: An Experiment 73
4.3 What Factors Affect the Rate of Evaporation?: An Experiment 81
4.4 Isolating Gaseous Nitrogen: A Demonstration 88

Chapter 5

Population Cycles 95

5.1 Population Cycle: A Model 97
5.2 Human World Population: An Analysis 101

Glossary 107
Appendix: Science Supply Companies 109
Further Reading and Internet Addresses 110
Index 111

Indicates experiments that offer ideas for science fair projects.

Introduction

We live in a world of constant change. But many things come back to be the way they were. We say they make a cycle. For example, we see rain fall from clouds to the ground. At the same time, water is evaporating into the air as a gas. Eventually, the water in the air collects as tiny droplets forming clouds that give rise to rain. Then the rain falls back to Earth completing a cycle—the water cycle. In this book, you will learn more about the water cycle and other cycles as well. Some other cycles include the sun and seasons, and the oxygen, carbon, nitrogen, and phosphorus cycles.

These cycles are ongoing and natural, but the world's growing population and its activities, such as agriculture, industry, and energy production, can disturb all of Earth's cycles. For example, burning fossil fuels (coal, oil, and natural gas) has affected the carbon cycle. Since the beginning of the Industrial Revolution, the burning of fossil fuels has increased, adding nearly 40 percent more carbon dioxide to the atmosphere. Carbon dioxide is a greenhouse gas. It reflects heat radiated by the earth back toward the ground. The boost in the amount of carbon dioxide and other greenhouse gases in the atmosphere has caused Earth to slowly grow warmer. A changing world climate, together with Earth's exploding human population, puts great pressure on our limited supply of water, soil, food, and other resources.

To confront this problem, we need to work toward a "greener" world. By "green" we mean actions that are good for, or do not harm, the environment.

As you read, you will examine some of Earth's natural cycles and the effects that human activities have on them. You will do so by reading, doing experiments to test a hypothesis, making models to illustrate ideas, carrying out demonstrations to better understand concepts, or making measurements. You will discover, too, what you can do to make a greener Earth.

The Scientific Method

Scientists look at the world and try to understand how things work. They make careful observations and conduct research. Different areas of science use different approaches. Depending on the problem, one method is likely to be better than another. Designing a new medicine for heart disease, studying the spread of an invasive plant species such as purple loosestrife, and finding evidence of water on Mars require different methods.

Despite the differences, all scientists use a similar general approach in doing experiments. It is called the scientific method. In most experiments, some or all of the following steps are used: making an observation, formulating a question, making a hypothesis (an answer to the question) and a prediction (an if-then statement), designing and conducting an experiment, analyzing results and drawing conclusions, and accepting or rejecting the hypothesis. Scientists then share their findings by writing articles that are published in journals.

You might wonder how to start an experiment. When you observe something in the world, you may become curious and ask a question. Your question, which could come from an earlier experiment or from reading, may be answered by a well-designed investigation. Once you have a question, you can make a hypothesis. Your hypothesis is a possible answer to the question (what you think will happen). Once you have a hypothesis, it is time to design an experiment that will test a consequence of your hypothesis.

In most cases, you should do a controlled experiment. This means having two groups that are treated the same except for the one factor being tested. That factor is called the variable. For example, suppose your question is "Do green plants need light?" You would use two groups of green plants. One group is called the control group; the other is called the experimental group. The two groups should be treated the same except for one factor. Both should be planted in the same amount and type of soil, given the same amount of water, kept at the same temperature, and so forth. The control group should be placed in the dark. The experimental group should be placed in the light. Light is the variable. It is the only difference between the two groups.

During the experiment, you will collect data. For example, you may measure the plant's growth in centimeters, count the number of living and dead leaves, and note the color and condition of the leaves. By comparing the data collected from the control and experimental groups over a few weeks, you may be able to draw conclusions. Healthier growth and survival rates of plants grown in light would allow you to conclude that green plants need light.

Two other terms are often used in scientific experiments—*dependent* and *independent variables*. One dependent variable in this example is healthy growth, which depends on light being present. Light is the independent variable. It doesn't depend on anything. After the data is collected, it is analyzed to see if it supports or rejects the hypothesis. The results of one experiment often lead you to a related question. Or they may send you off in a different direction. Whatever the results, something can be learned from every experiment.

At times, as you carry out the activities in this book, you may need a partner to help you. It is best to work with someone who enjoys experimenting as much as you do. That way you will both enjoy what you are doing. If any safety issues are involved in doing an experiment, you will be warned. In some cases, to avoid danger, you will be asked to work with an adult. Please do so. We don't want you to take any chances that could lead to an injury.

Like any good scientist, you will find it useful to record your ideas, notes, data, and anything you can conclude from your investigations in a notebook. By doing so, you can keep track of the information you gather and the conclusions you reach. Your notebook will allow you to refer back to things you have done and help you in doing other projects in the future.

Science Fairs

Some of the investigations in this book contain ideas that may lead you to a science fair project. Those project ideas are indicated with a symbol (✓). However, judges at science fairs do not reward projects or experiments that are simply copied from a book. For example, a diagram of the water cycle would not impress most judges; however, an experiment showing the effect of clouds on global warming would be more likely to get their attention.

Science fair judges reward creative thought and imagination. It is difficult to be creative or imaginative unless you are really interested in your project. So try to choose an investigation that excites you. And before you jump into a project, consider your own talents and the cost of the materials you will need.

If you use an experiment or idea from this book for a science fair, find ways to modify or extend it. This should not be difficult. As you carry out investigations, new ideas will come to mind. You will think of questions that experiments can answer. The experiments will make excellent science fair projects, particularly because the ideas are your own and are interesting to you.

If you decide to enter a science fair and have never done so, read some of the books listed in the Further Reading section. These books deal specifically with science fairs. They provide plenty of helpful hints and useful information. The books will help you avoid the pitfalls that sometimes plague first-time entrants. You will learn how to prepare appealing reports that include charts and graphs, set up and display your work, present your project, and relate to judges and visitors.

Safety First

Safety is important in science, and certain rules apply when doing experiments. Some of the rules below may seem obvious to you, others may not, but it is important that you follow all of them.

1. Have **an adult** help you whenever the book advises.
2. Wear eye protection and closed-toe shoes (not sandals). Tie back long hair.
3. Do not eat or drink while experimenting. Never taste substances being used (unless instructed to do so).
4. Do not touch chemicals.
5. The liquid in some thermometers is mercury (a dense liquid metal). It is dangerous to touch mercury or breathe mercury vapor, and such thermometers have been banned in many states. When doing these experiments, use only non-mercury thermometers, such as those filled with alcohol. If you have a mercury thermometer in the house, **ask an adult** if it can be taken to a local thermometer exchange location.
6. Do only those experiments that are described in the book or those that have been approved by **an adult**.

7. Maintain a serious attitude while conducting experiments. Never engage in horseplay or play practical jokes.
8. Before beginning an experiment, read all of the instructions carefully and be sure you understand them.
9. Remove all items not needed for the experiment from your work space.
10. At the end of every activity, clean all materials used and put them away. Then wash your hands thoroughly with soap and water.

Chapter 1

The Solar Cycle: Sustaining All Other Cycles

There are many chemicals essential to life. Water, carbon, oxygen, phosphorus, and nitrogen are a few of them. These chemicals go through natural cycles that carry them through the atmosphere, the earth, and living organisms. There is a carbon cycle, a water cycle, a nitrogen cycle, and more. With the exception of the small amount of matter that reaches the earth as meteorites or comets, the world's total mass of chemicals stays the same. Although the amount of these substances in each phase of a cycle stays the same, they can be upset by human actions. In this chapter, we examine the cycle that makes all other Earth cycles possible: the solar cycle.

The sun sets in the western sky as part of its daily cycle.

The Solar Cycle

The sun goes through a daily and an annual cycle. Earth's closest star is only 150,000,000 kilometers (93,000,000 miles) away. You may not think 150,000,000 kilometers is very close. After all, it takes light, which travels at 300,000 kilometers per second (186,000 mi/s), more than eight minutes to travel from the sun to Earth. However, the distance to the next closest star is 40 trillion kilometers (25 trillion miles). It takes light from that star, Alpha Centauri, more than four years to reach us.

To see the sun's daily and annual cycle, you will need to know directions (north, south, east, and west). You will use these directions together with altitude to locate the sun in the sky. You will find that the sun's path across the sky changes. People say the sun rises in the east. But, the location of the sunrise is not the same every day. The sun rises in the direction we call due east only twice each year. On other days, it rises somewhat north or south of due east.

1.1 Directions from a Shadow Cast by the Midday Sun: A Measurement

Things YOU will Need:

- flat, open area where you can draw lines or place stones on the ground
- local newspaper, Web site, or TV weather station that gives the time of sunrise and sunset
- watch or clock
- straight stick
- hammer
- carpenter's level
- string
- big nail
- small stones
- tape measure

You can find the direction called north using a stick and the sun at midday.

1. Find an open, level area where you can place stones or scratch lines on the ground. If possible, find a place near where you can also watch the sun rise and set.
2. Use a local daily newspaper, Web site, or TV weather station to find the time of sunrise and sunset for each day in a nearby city or town. Midday occurs midway between

sunrise and sunset. It rarely occurs at exactly noon (12 P.M.). Knowing the exact time of midday will be helpful, but it is also the time when the day's shadows are shortest.

3. To find the time of midday, determine the total time between sunrise and sunset and divide it by 2. Add that time to the time of sunrise to find midday. For example, if sunrise is at 6:21 A.M. and sunset is 5:31 P.M., the total length of the day is the sum of 5 hours and 39 minutes (6:21 A.M. to 12:00 P.M.) plus 5 hours and 31 minutes (12:00 P.M. to 5:31 P.M.), which equals 10 hours and 70 minutes or 11 hours and 10 minutes. Half of 11 hours and 10 minutes is 5 hours and 35 minutes. The approximate time of midday then will be the time of sunrise plus 5 hours and 35 minutes or 5:35 + 6:21 = 11:56. Midday would be four minutes before noon. At this time, shadows will reach their shortest length because the sun will be at its highest point in the sky.
4. About half an hour before midday on a sunny day, go outside and hammer a stick into the ground. The stick should be vertical (straight up and down). Use a carpenter's level to make sure the stick is vertical.
5. In case there may be clouds when midday arrives, tie a loop at one end of a string. Slide the loop over and to the bottom of the vertical stick. Stretch the string along the stick's shadow. Put a big nail at the end of the stick's shadow and hold it firmly against the stretched string. Use the length of the stick's shadow as the radius of a circle.
6. Use the string and nail to draw an arc (a partial circle) around the stick as shown in Figure 1a.
7. Mark the spot where the end of the shadow touches the circle with a small stone.

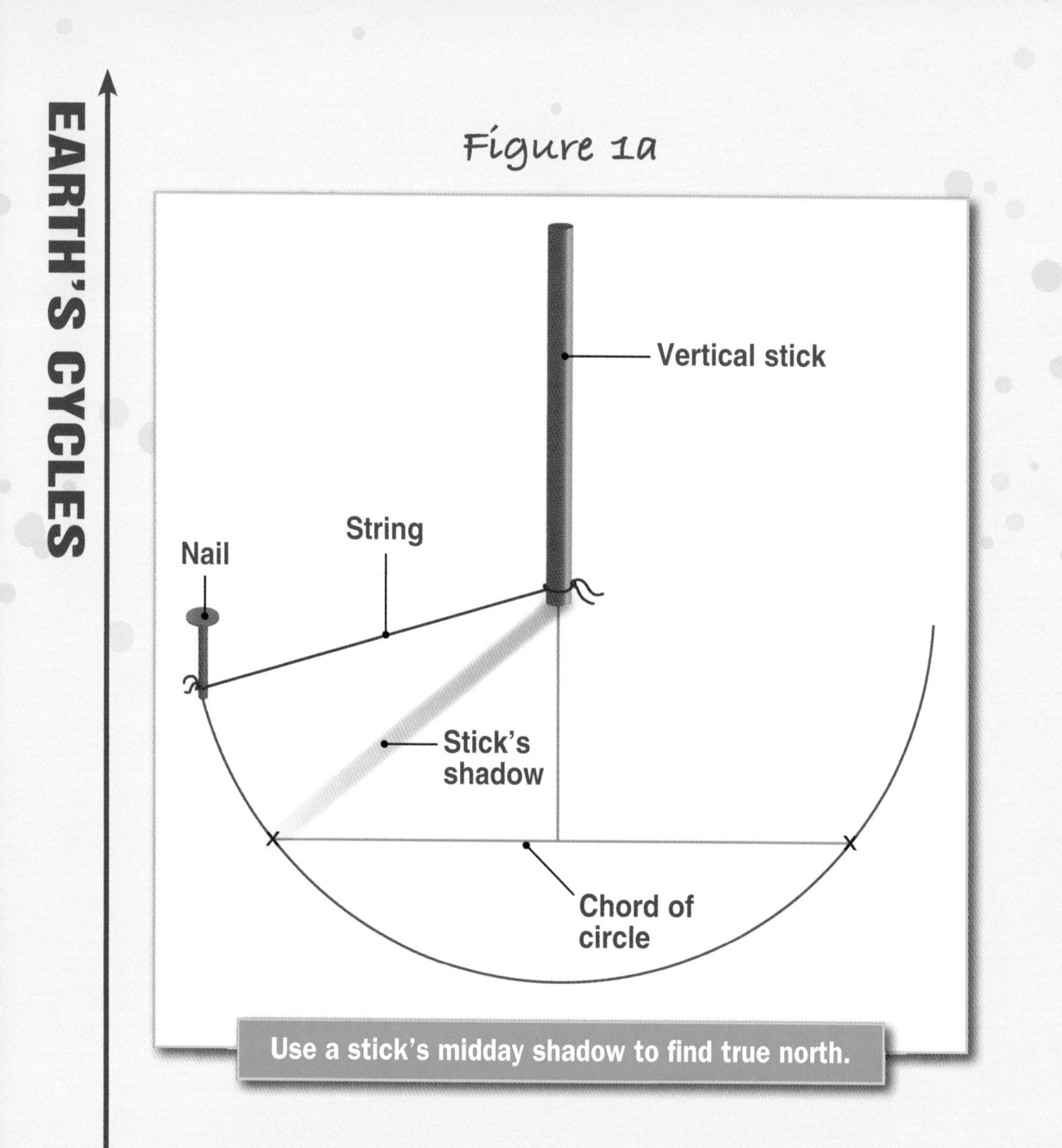

Use a stick's midday shadow to find true north.

8. As midday approaches, the shadow will grow shorter. If the sun is shining at midday, mark the end of the shadow with a stone. This will be the stick's shortest shadow. The shadow points north. Draw or mark a line along this shadow.

You can skip to step 12.

9. If the sun is behind a cloud at midday, wait. If the sun reappears after midday, the stick's shadow will continue to move but grow longer. When the shadow again touches the circle, mark that spot with another small stone.

10. Scratch a straight line connecting the two small stones. Using a tape measure, mark the middle of the line you just drew. Then draw a second line from the base of the stick to the midpoint of the first line you just marked. This second line points toward true north (see Figure 1b.). It will lie along what was the stick's shortest shadow.

11. Put a second stick at the center of the first line you drew. This point would have been where the end of the stick's

Figure 1b

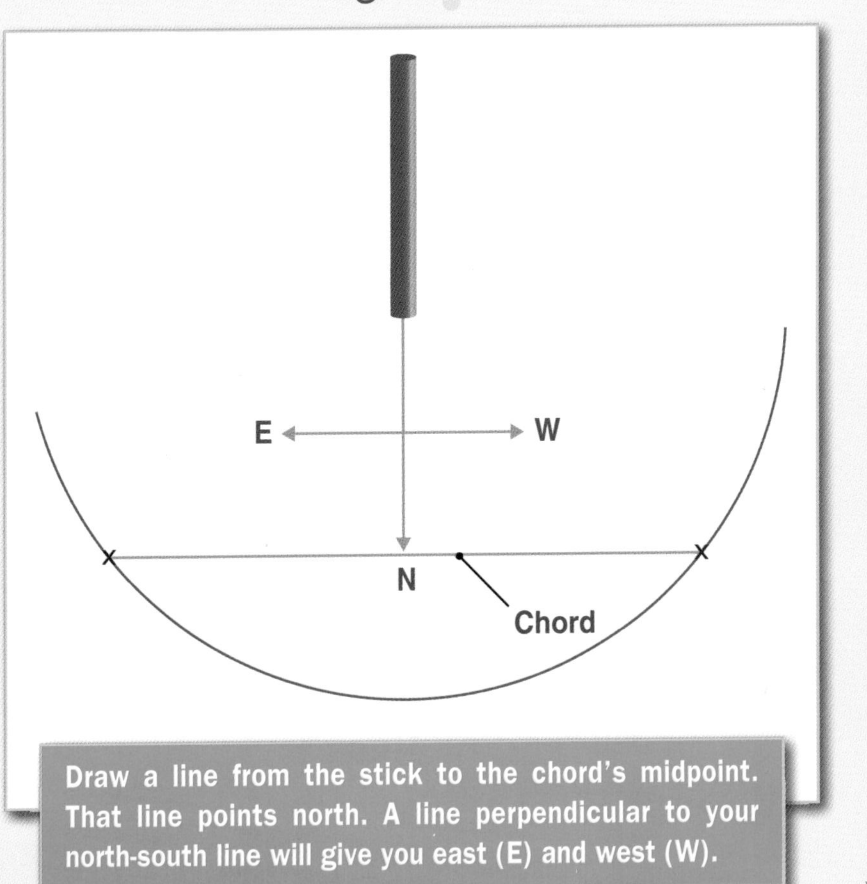

Draw a line from the stick to the chord's midpoint. That line points north. A line perpendicular to your north-south line will give you east (E) and west (W).

midday shadow fell. The direction of a line from the first stick to the second is true north. How can you find the direction we call south?

12. To find east and west, stand on the north-south line and face north. Raise your right arm away from the side of your body and extend your index finger. It will point east. Raise your left arm the same way. Your left index finger will point west.

To make an east-west line on the ground, simply scratch a line perpendicular to the north-south line. You can label the ends of this line *E* (east) and *W* (west).

13. To make the north-south and east-west lines more permanent, mark the lines on the ground with small stones or stretch heavy string between sticks driven into the ground at the ends of the two lines.

Ideas for Science Fair Projects

- Use the stick and its shortest shadow to find the altitude of the midday sun.
- Measure the sun's midday altitude at different times of the year. When is it at its maximum altitude? When is it at its minimum altitude?
- Use a watch and the shadow of a toothpick on the watch to roughly find north.

1.2 Checking Your North-South Line:
A Measurement

Polaris (the North Star) lies almost directly above Earth's North Pole, it can be used to check the north line you made in Measurement 1.1.

1. On a clear night, stand on the south end of the north-south line you made. Look for Polaris in the northern sky. The stars of the Big Dipper can help you find Polaris. The Big Dipper is a group of stars that looks like a ladle (Figure 2). (If you live in a very southern part of the United States, the Big Dipper may not be visible during the summer.) The Big Dipper may be turned at a different angle than the one shown in Figure 2. It can be in any of the positions you see when you slowly turn Figure 2 all the way around. Merak and Dubhe (see Figure 2) serve as pointer stars. They point toward Polaris.
2. With your arm extended, put your thumb and index finger "on" these two stars of the Big Dipper. Imagine a line connecting Merak to Dubhe. Keeping your fingers at the same separation, imagine extending that line 5 times

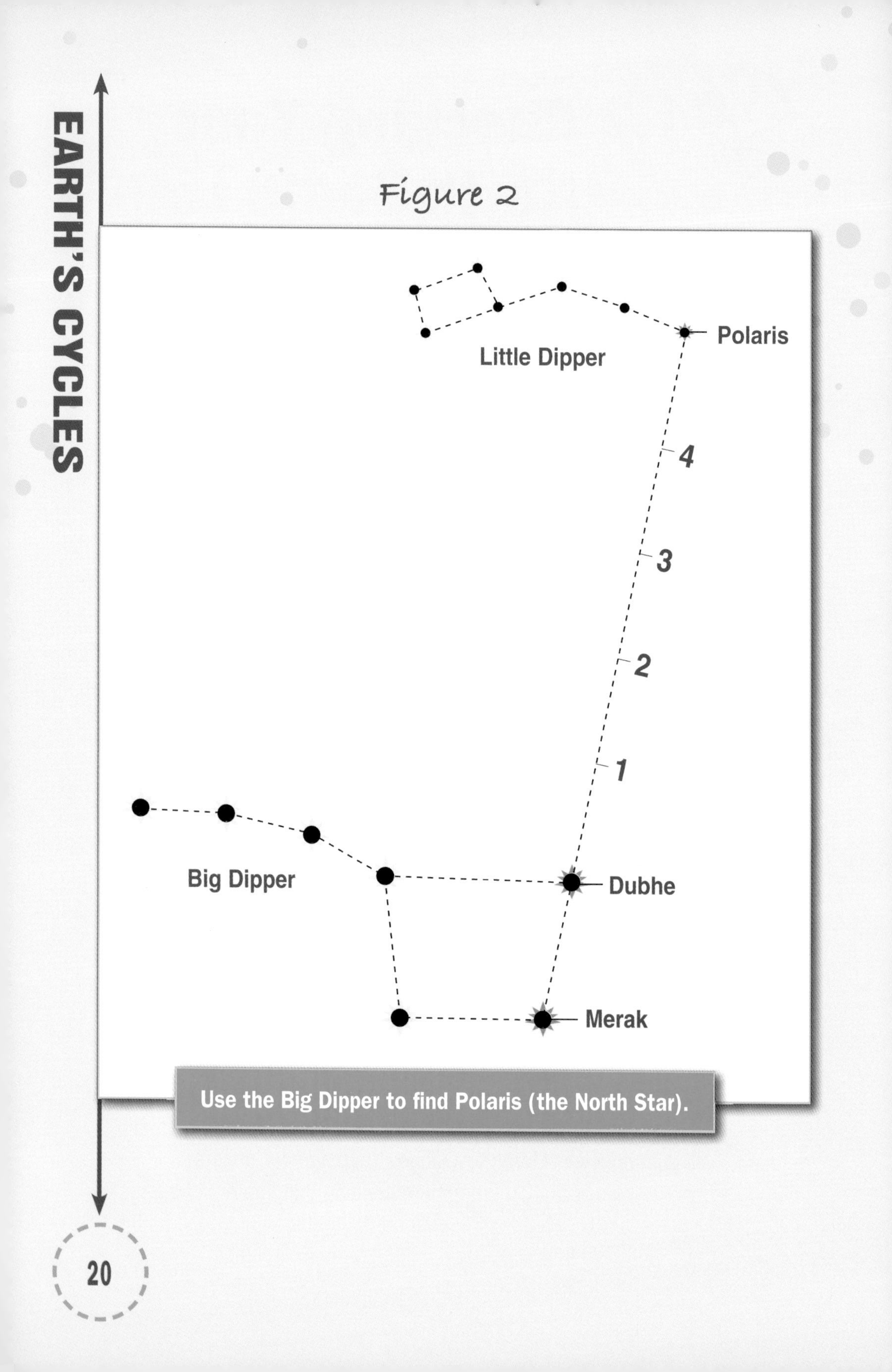

Use the Big Dipper to find Polaris (the North Star).

longer. At the end of that line you will find Polaris. It is the last star on the handle of the Little Dipper (see Figure 2).

The direction north is under the North Star, which is almost directly above Earth's North Pole.

3. Point at the North Star. The north-south line you made with two sticks should be under your arm.
4. Compare your north-south line with north as indicated by a magnetic compass. Does the compass agree with your north-south line or the direction of Polaris?

   Don't be surprised if north according to the compass doesn't agree with your north-south line. Earth's magnetic poles are not at its geographic poles. Earth's northern magnetic pole is near latitude 83° north and longitude 114° west in northern Canada. This pole has been moving about 40 kilometers (25 miles) per year. On Cape Cod in Massachusetts, a compass needle points about 17° west of true north. In what direction does your compass needle point?

Ideas for Science Fair Projects

- **Observe the Big Dipper at approximately the same time in the evening at least once a month. What happens to its position in the sky? Try to explain why the Big Dipper changes position and Polaris does not.**
- **Try to identify other constellations in the northern sky, such as Cassiopeia, Cepheus, Draco, and Mizar. Do these constellations change position over time?**
- **Show why Earth's magnetic pole in northern Canada must be a south magnetic pole.**

1.3 Find Two Cycles of the Sun by Watching Sunrise and Sunset:

Observations

Now that you know the directions, you can observe the sun's two cycles.

1. Over the course of a year, wake up early on or around the twentieth of each month (more often if you can) and watch the sunrise. A local newspaper, Web site, or TV weather station will give the time of sunrise so you can set an alarm clock if necessary.
2. Use the directional lines you made in Measurement 1.1 to locate the direction of the sun as it rises. **Never look directly at the sun.** It can damage your eyes. Record the date and the direction of the rising sun each time you observe sunrise. To estimate degrees north or south of east, you can use your fists. A fist at arm's length covers very nearly 10 degrees of the sky. (See Figure 3a.)

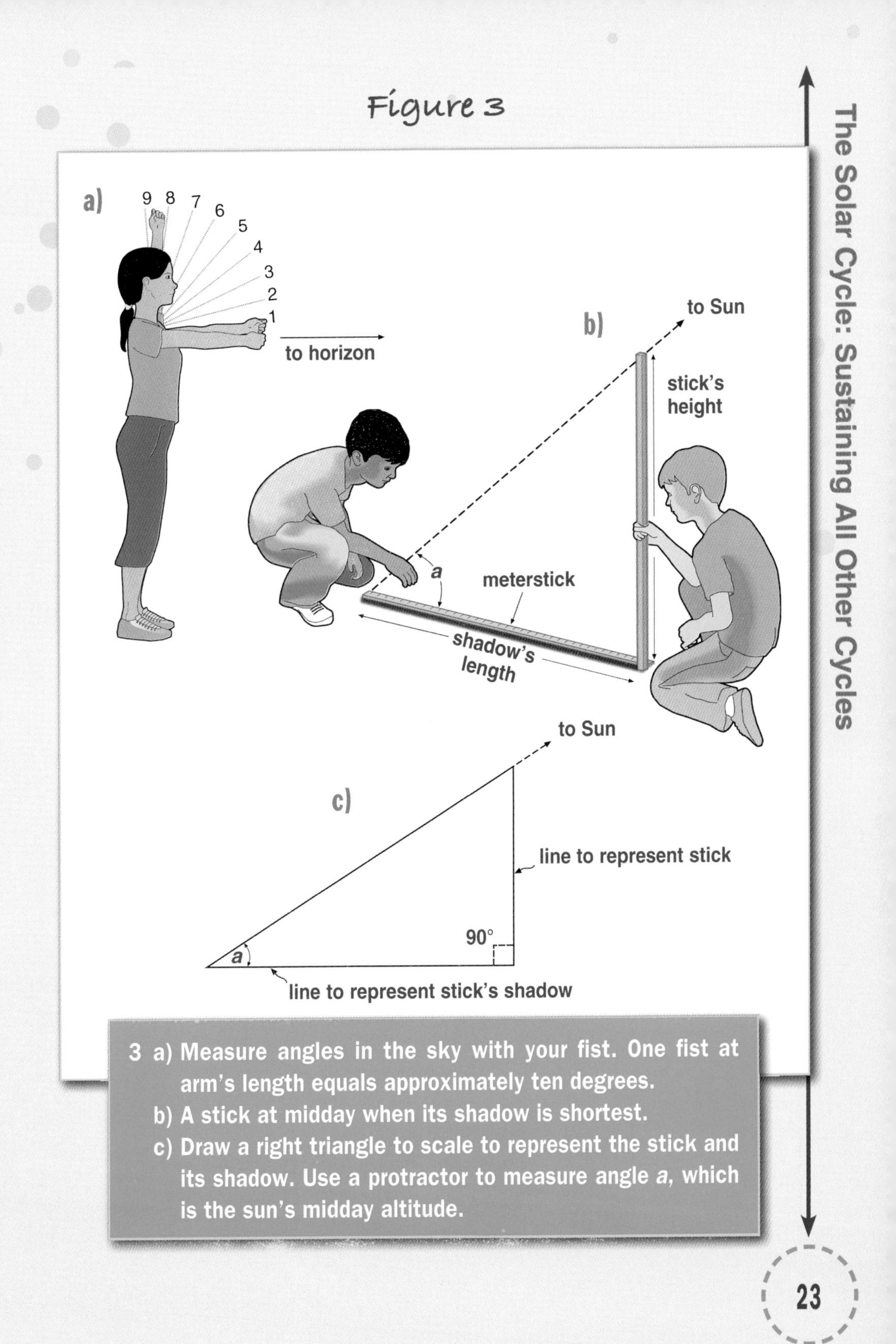

3 a) Measure angles in the sky with your fist. One fist at arm's length equals approximately ten degrees.
b) A stick at midday when its shadow is shortest.
c) Draw a right triangle to scale to represent the stick and its shadow. Use a protractor to measure angle *a*, which is the sun's midday altitude.

3. On the days you watch the sunrise, measure the vertical stick and the length of its shadow at midday. Use your measurements to find the sun's altitude at midday as shown in Figures 3b and 3c. Record the date and the altitude.
4. Use your directional lines on the days you watch the sunrise to locate the direction to the sun as it sets. Record the date and the direction of the setting sun each time you observe sunset.

What daily cycle of the sun have you observed? What seasonal cycle of the sun have you observed? Over the course of one year, what annual cycle have you seen? What happens to the sun's midday altitude over the course of a year?

Using the Sun to Make a Greener Earth

The sun is a key factor in making Earth greener. Most of Earth is bathed in sunlight at least part of each day. And sunlight is a source of energy. When the sun shines on photovoltaic cells, light energy is converted to electrical energy. That energy can be used to run electrical devices, including lights and heating devices that warm our homes. As more of Earth's surface becomes covered with solar panels, such as those in the photograph below, we will need to burn less fossil fuel to generate electricity. By burning fewer fossil fuels we can reduce the amount of carbon dioxide emitted in the atmosphere and reduce global warming. This will create a greener atmosphere.

The photovoltaic cells in these solar panels can convert light energy from the sun into electrical energy.

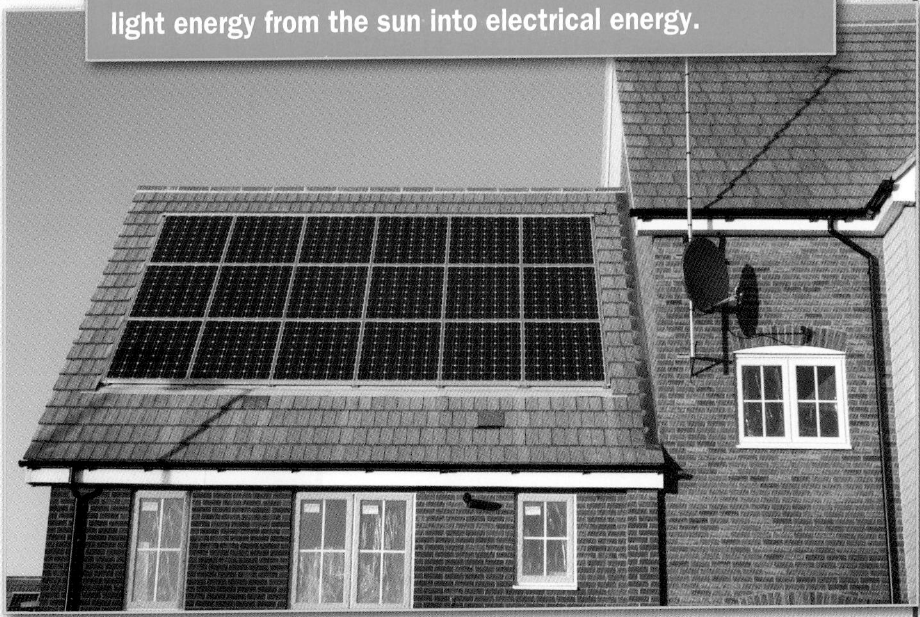

1.4 Mapping the Sun's Path Across the Sky: An Experiment

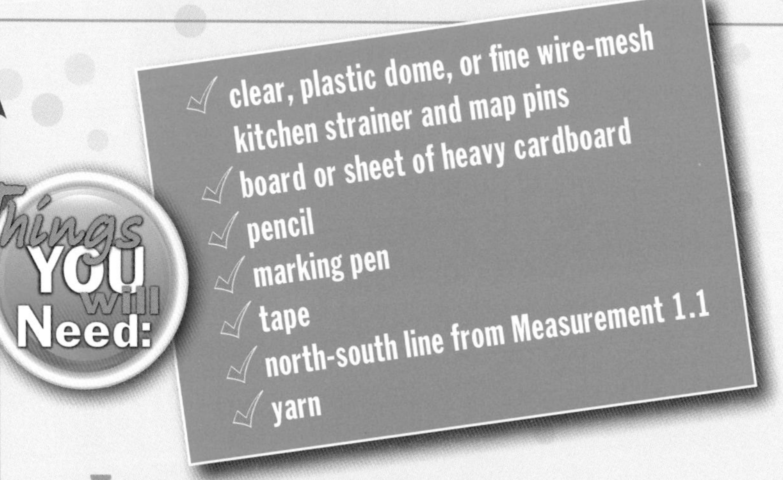

Look at the sky. It appears to be a huge dome with you at its center. The dome you see is half of the spherical sky that surrounds Earth. Astronomers call it the *celestial sphere*. You can see only one-half of the sphere—one hemisphere of sky. Someone on the opposite side of Earth will see the other hemisphere.

The stars, moon, planets, and our sun all seem to move across the celestial sphere every day.

What do you think will be the sun's path across the sky? How do you think the sun's path will change over the course of a year? Make a hypothesis. Then do this experiment.

1. To map the sun's path, you will need a clear, plastic dome to represent the celestial hemisphere. Put the dome or strainer on a board or a sheet of heavy cardboard (Figure 4). Mark the dome's circular base with a pencil.

Figure 4

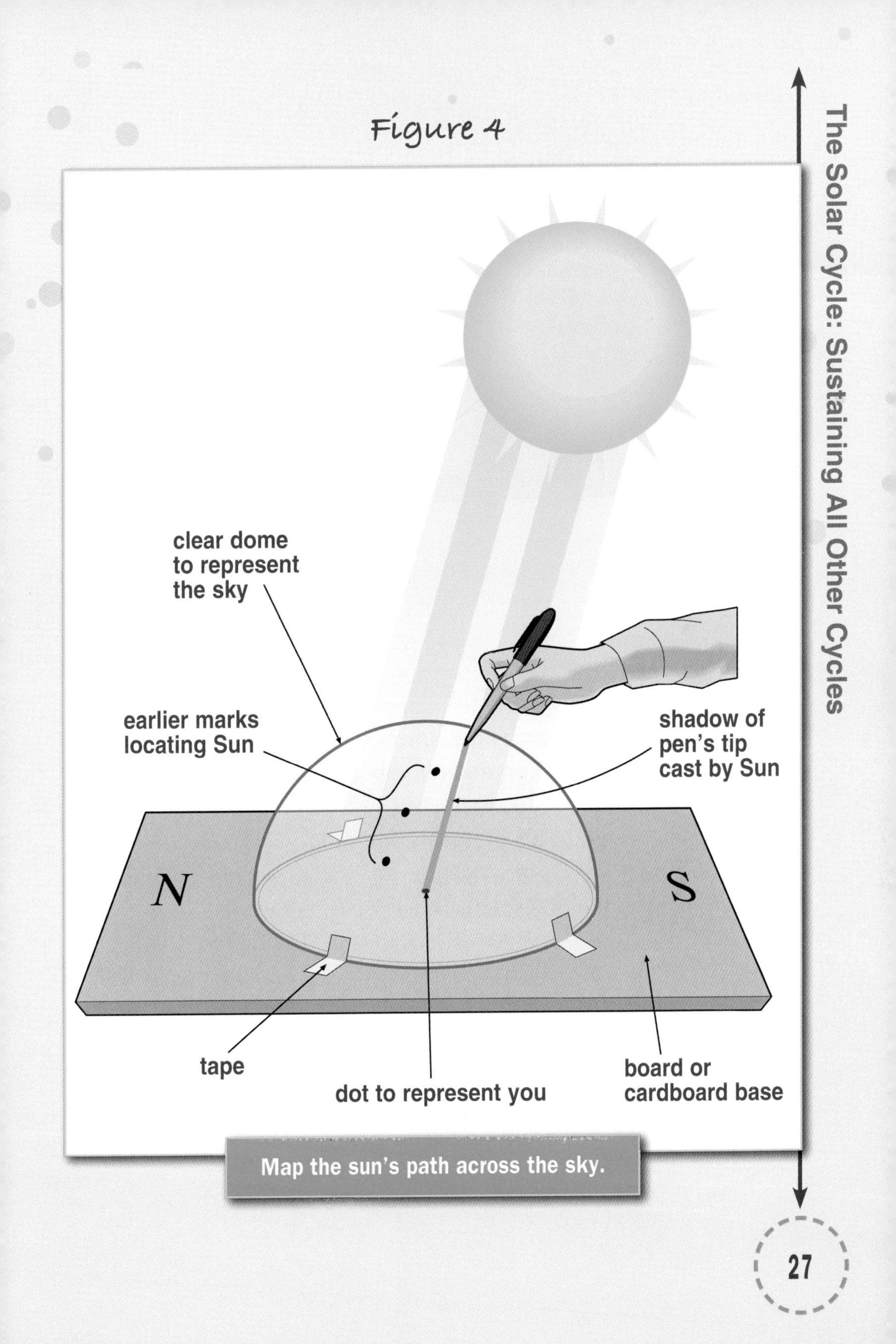

Map the sun's path across the sky.

2. Remove the hemisphere. Use a marking pen to make a dot at the exact center of the circle. The dot represents you at the center of the celestial hemisphere. Put the dome or strainer back in its original position. Tape it to its base.
3. Starting as near sunrise as possible, place the base where it will be in the sun all day. If possible, place it on the north-south line you made in Measurement 1.1. Be sure the base is level. Mark the outline of the base so that if it is accidentally moved it can be replaced in its exact position.
4. Use the north-south line to orient the dome. Make an "N" on the base so that you can put the dome in the same position when you repeat this experiment later.
5. Mark the sun's position in the sky with a marking pen as shown in Figure 4. Place the tip of the marking pen on the dome so that the tip's shadow falls on the dot at the dome's center. (If you use a strainer, map pins can be used to cast shadows and colorfully mark the sun's path.) The mark you make will be in line with the sun and the center of the dome.
6. Try to mark the sun's position every hour or more often during the time the sun is in the sky. By the end of the day, you will have a permanent map of the sun's path across the sky on that day of the year.
7. Try to do this experiment at least four times, more often if you can. The four most important dates to map the sun are on or around March 21, June 21, September 21, and December 21.

When is the sun's path highest and longest across the sky? When is its path lowest and shortest? On what dates are the paths the same?

1.5 How Earth Creates the Apparent Cycles of the Sun: Models

You know that the sun rises and sets each day, a daily cycle. You have also seen that the sun appears to move gradually higher in the sky from late December until late June, making an increasingly longer and higher path across the sky. The sun's higher, longer path supplies more energy to Earth. From late June until late December, the sun appears to gradually move lower in the sky, making an increasingly shorter path across the sky.

A simple model easily explains the sun's daily cycle. Its annual cycle requires a more complex model. You can make models of both cycles.

The Daily Cycle

1. Turn on a single lightbulb in a dark room. The lightbulb represents the sun. Stick a toothpick into a white foam ball. The ball represents Earth. Use the toothpick as "Earth's" South Pole and as a handle. Hold the ball a few feet from the lightbulb. You will see that the side of the ball facing the lightbulb is in "sunlight." The side away from the "sun" is dark.
2. Slowly rotate the ball on its axis as shown in Figure 5a. The side that was formerly in darkness slowly becomes bathed in "sunlight." As you see, the daily rising and setting of the sun is caused by a rotating Earth.

The Annual Cycle

1. Figure 5b shows that Earth's axis is tilted relative to the plane of its orbit around the sun. Using the white foam ball, move the ball about the lightbulb as shown in Figure 5b. Because Earth's axis is tilted, its northern hemisphere receives more light than the southern hemisphere when Earth is at one side of its orbit. When it is at the opposite side, the southern hemisphere receives more light than the northern hemisphere. In between, both hemispheres receive equal amounts of light.

   When the North Pole is tilted toward the sun (position I in Figure 5b), the sun is higher in the sky and the northern hemisphere has its summer. When the North Pole is tilted away from the sun (position III in Figure 5b), the sun's path is lower in the sky; the northern hemisphere has its winter. When the hemispheres receive equal amounts of light (positions II and IV in Figure 5b), Earth is at its spring or autumn equinox.

Figure 5

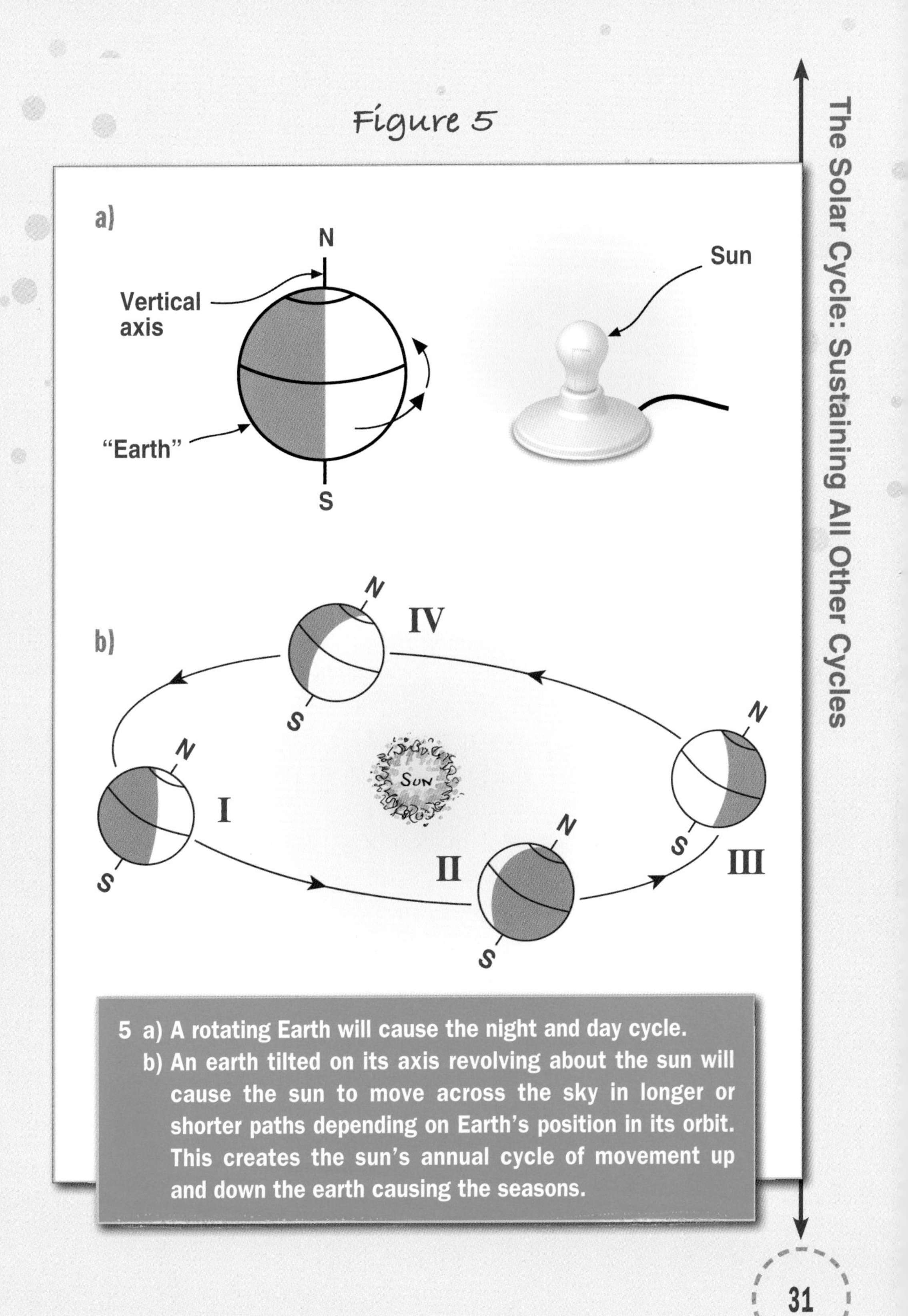

5 a) A rotating Earth will cause the night and day cycle.
b) An earth tilted on its axis revolving about the sun will cause the sun to move across the sky in longer or shorter paths depending on Earth's position in its orbit. This creates the sun's annual cycle of movement up and down the earth causing the seasons.

Ideas for Science Fair Projects

- How did the French scientist Jean Foucault (1819–1868) prove that it is the earth's rotation that causes the sun's daily cycle and not the sun revolving about Earth?
- Use your model to show why the North Pole is in darkness during winter in the northern hemisphere.

Earth's Orbit

Earth's orbit around the sun is not a perfect circle. It is slightly elliptical (oval-shaped), and the distance between Earth and sun changes slightly. Earth is at perihelion (closest to the sun) in early January when it is about 147 million kilometers (91.4 million miles) from the sun. It is at aphelion (farthest from the sun) in early July when the sun is about 152 million kilometers (94.5 million miles) from Earth. As you can see, our distance from the sun does not change very much (3.3%).

Earth's average speed along its orbit is 29.8 kilometers per second (18.6 mi/s). Its speed is slightly greater when it is closer to the sun and slightly less when it is farther from the sun. Therefore, Earth moves a bit faster around the sun during the northern hemisphere's winter and slightly slower during its summer. That is why there are 179 days from the autumn equinox (around September 20) to the spring equinox (around March 20), but 186 days from the spring equinox to the autumn equinox.

You may wonder how we can be closest to the sun in winter and farthest from the sun in summer. (If you lived south of the equator where the seasons are reversed, you probably would not wonder about this fact.) The next experiment will help you understand why the difference in the sun's distance is less important than its position above the earth.

1.6 Season Cycles and the Sun: Models

Things YOU will Need:

- sheet of paper
- table
- dark room
- flashlight
- globe marked with tropics of Capricorn and Cancer

From your maps of the sun's path across the sky, you know the sun is higher in the sky on the first day of summer than at any other time of the year. During the winter, the sun is much lower in the sky, and its light falls on Earth at a lower angle. Make a model to see what effect the seasonal path of the sun has on the heat it delivers to Earth's surface.

1. Place a sheet of paper on a table in a dark room. The paper represents a portion of Earth's surface.
2. Shine a flashlight directly down onto the paper from above. Then tip the flashlight so that its light strikes the paper at a much lower angle.

What happens to the area covered by the light from the flashlight? How has the amount of light per area changed? How does this affect the heat delivered to this part of the earth?

3. Replace the paper with a globe. At the beginning of winter in the northern hemisphere (around December 21), the

Figure 6

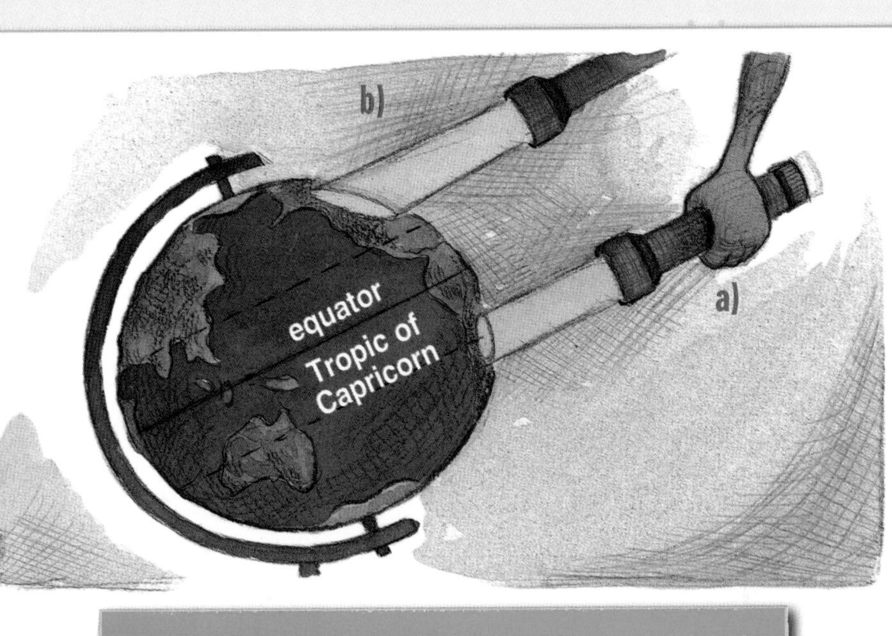

Light from the "sun" shining directly on a globe's tropic of Capricorn is less spread out than the same "sun" shining on the globe's United States.

sun is directly above the tropic of Capricorn, which is located 23.5 degrees south of the equator (see Figure 6a). Shine the flashlight on the globe perpendicular to the tropic of Capricorn. Slowly move the flashlight upward keeping it tilted parallel to its original angle until the light shines on the United States (see Figure 6b).

What happens when the light is shining on the United States? Does the light cover more, the same, or less area than it did when it was shining on the tropic of Capricorn?

The sun's light heats Earth. How will the sun's energy delivered to the United States compare with the heat delivered to the same area along the tropic of Capricorn on December 21?

4. At the beginning of summer, around June 21, the sun will be directly over the tropic of Cancer. Repeat the experiment, but this time shine the light perpendicular to the tropic of Cancer, 23.5 degrees north of the equator.

How does the amount of light per area striking the United States in summer compare with the amount per area in winter?

Ideas for Science Fair Projects

Remove a globe from its holder. Put the globe on a large, opened tin can in bright sunlight. Orient the globe so that where you live is uppermost and the globe's north pole points north. Stick a pin through a short length of a cut-off drinking straw. Hold the straw perpendicular to the globe's surface. You should be able to find the latitude where the sun is presently directly overhead and the straw casts no shadow. The sun's path should be along that latitude all day.

Continue this experiment over the course of six months or longer. What happens to the sun's position relative to Earth's surface?

The Carbon and Oxygen Cycles

Like water, carbon and oxygen are essential for life. Carbon is in all organic compounds, including the DNA in our cells and all the foods we eat. Most of our carbon came from Earth's interior. It comes to the surface as carbon dioxide gas from volcanoes. Carbon dioxide makes up about 0.04 percent of the atmosphere. It is one of the greenhouse gases that helps keep Earth warm by reflecting heat back to the ground.

Carbon, like the sun, moves through cycles, from the air to living tissue to the earth and back to the atmosphere (Figure 7). Individual carbon molecules may pass through the cycle quickly or, as in the case of fossil fuels, over millions of years.

Plants play a vital role in the carbon cycle. They use the sun's energy, together with substances available in Earth's atmosphere and ground, to manufacture most of the world's food. The process is called photosynthesis. During photosynthesis, green plants

Figure 7

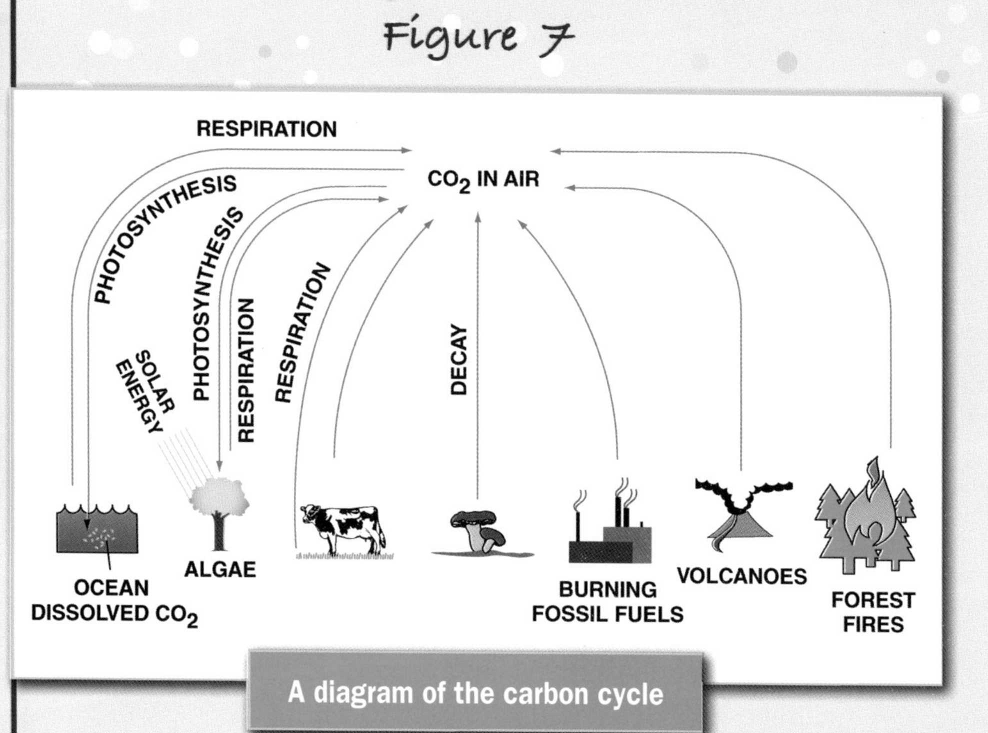

A diagram of the carbon cycle

combine carbon dioxide from the air with water from the ground to make carbohydrates, a vital source of food and energy. The chemical equation below summarizes the process of photosynthesis.

$$\underset{\text{carbon dioxide}}{6\,CO_2} + \underset{\text{water}}{6\,H_2O} + \text{light and chlorophyll} \rightarrow \underset{\text{sugar}}{2C_3H_6O_3} + \underset{\text{oxygen}}{6O_2}$$

The chemical reactions involved in photosynthesis are powered by light energy. The light is absorbed by the green pigment chlorophyll, which accounts for the color of many plants. The carbon compounds found in plant cells are transferred to animals when they eat the plants.

During respiration, plants and animals take in oxygen. The oxygen combines with foods, such as glucose sugar, to provide the energy needed to do work and carry on life. The overall chemical reaction between glucose, a simple sugar, and oxygen is shown by the chemical equation below.

$$\underset{\text{glucose}}{C_6H_{12}O_6} + \underset{\text{oxygen}}{6O_2} \rightarrow \underset{\text{carbon dioxide}}{6\,CO_2} + \underset{\text{water}}{6\,H_2O} + \text{Energy}$$

The carbon in glucose becomes the carbon in carbon dioxide (CO_2). Humans and other animals produce carbon dioxide during respiration. The gas enters the blood stream and is carried to the lungs, where it is exhaled.

Some of the carbon dioxide released during respiration is used in photosynthesis to make food. Similarly, some of the oxygen released during photosynthesis is used in respiration. During daylight, photosynthesis produces more oxygen than is required for animal respiration. The excess oxygen diffuses from leaves into the air. At night, lacking light, photosynthesis stops, but respiration continues. Animals breathe in the excess oxygen generated during the day. This way, the oxygen content of the air remains constant.

When organisms die, they decompose (break down) and produce carbon dioxide. The carbon dioxide is released back into the atmosphere. Sometimes before decay is complete dead plants, animals, and bacteria are covered by additional dead matter. Over millions of years, as layers of dead matter built up, the pressure produced fossil fuels—coal, oil, and natural gas. All fossil fuels contain the carbon originally in the cells of ancient plants and animals. In the case of oil, which lies in pockets deep inside the earth, the decay process results in hydrocarbons (liquid compounds made up of carbon and hydrogen), such as octane (C_8H_{18}). Natural gas is produced in a similar manner. Its hydrocarbons are smaller, lighter molecules, such as methane (CH_4). Coal is a solid that is primarily carbon, a black element.

When fossil fuels are burned, they too produce carbon dioxide that is returned to the atmosphere. For example, coal, which is mostly carbon, burns in the presence of oxygen to produce carbon dioxide as shown by the reaction below.

$$C + O_2 \rightarrow CO_2 + \text{Energy}$$

All living cells take in oxygen and release carbon dioxide, which enters the atmosphere (or water in the case of aquatic organisms). Until recently the atmospheric concentration of gases remained relatively constant. The atmosphere is 21 percent oxygen and 78 percent nitrogen. Other gases make up about 1 percent. Over the last 250 years, humans have been burning increasing amounts fossil fuels. As a result, the carbon dioxide concentration in our atmosphere has increased.

Global Warming and the Carbon Cycle

Sunlight is made up of a variety of wavelengths. The wavelengths of visible light range from 0.0004 mm (violet light) to 0.0007 mm (red light). We cannot see wavelengths that are not part of this scale. Shorter wavelengths include ultraviolet light. Longer wavelengths include infrared light.

Our atmosphere contains a number of greenhouse gases, such as carbon dioxide, methane, and nitrogen oxides. Greenhouse gases in the atmosphere act like a greenhouse. They trap heat. They allow the shorter wavelengths of sunlight to pass through the air. But they reflect back to Earth some of the longer wavelengths that would otherwise leave Earth and escape to outer space. These longer wavelengths carry heat. If these waves were not reflected back to the ground, Earth would be much colder than it is. But because of the increased amount of greenhouse gases, Earth is becoming warmer. Carbon dioxide is the most abundant greenhouse gas in our atmosphere.

Since the Industrial Revolution, humans have had a profound effect on the carbon cycle. During that time, the concentration of carbon dioxide in the atmosphere has increased by about 40 percent from 280 ppm (parts per million) to nearly 400 ppm. And the rate at which carbon dioxide levels are rising is increasing. Some scientists predict that atmospheric carbon dioxide will double by 2110 unless carbon dioxide levels are reduced.

Increased amounts of atmospheric carbon dioxide are the result of several factors. One factor is the cutting and burning of large tracts of tropical rain forests. These forests absorb vast amounts of carbon dioxide during photosynthesis and release corresponding quantities of oxygen. As these forests are cleared for logging, mining, roads, and agriculture, the carbon cycle is affected. Because there are fewer trees, less carbon dioxide is removed from the atmosphere. Also, these forests are burned during clearing. These fires add even more carbon dioxide to the atmosphere.

The major cause of increasing atmospheric carbon dioxide, however, is the use of fossil fuels to heat buildings and operate electric power plants, factories, and cars. Global use of fossil fuels sends about 25 billion tons of carbon dioxide into the air each year. Increasing levels of atmospheric carbon dioxide, the most abundant greenhouse gas in Earth's atmosphere, will continue to raise global temperatures. To reduce global warming, we need to lessen carbon dioxide production by slashing the use of fossil fuels.

Ocean Acidification

Increased amounts of carbon dioxide have affected Earth's oceans as well as its atmosphere. Carbon dioxide dissolves in water to form carbonic acid (H_2CO_3). The reaction between the gas and water is summarized by the chemical equation below.

$$CO_2 + H_2O \rightarrow H_2CO_3$$

Acidity is measured by pH. Acids have a pH less than 7; bases (alkalis) have a pH greater than 7. Normally, ocean water has a pH of 8.2, so it is basic, or alkaline. But because of the increased amount of carbon dioxide in the oceans, the pH of ocean water has dropped to nearly 8.0 and is continuing to fall. Both the increased ocean acidity and warm ocean temperatures are brought on by global warming. The combination is harming plant and animal life in the oceans, including coral reefs, which harbor an abundance of sea life.

Again, the solution is reducing the high level of carbon dioxide in the atmosphere. We need to scale down the burning of fossil fuels by developing renewable sources of energy—solar, wind, geothermal, and tidal.

2.1 Decomposition and Carbon: A Demonstration

Bacteria and fungi can decompose (break down) many kinds of organic matter, such as dead plants and animals. In this experiment, you will decompose matter by heating it. If the matter contains carbon, it will turn black when heated. How can you demonstrate which matter contains carbon? Let's find out.

1. Make a few shallow indentations about 3 centimeters (1 in) wide around the inside edge of two aluminum pie pans.
2. Put small pieces of substances that you think might contain carbon in the indentations in one pan. Try using sugar, baking soda, bread, apple, and potato. In the other pan, place substances that you suspect do not contain carbon, such as sand, gravel, steel washers, pennies, and aluminum foil.

3. Put on safety glasses. **Ask an adult** to wear safety glasses and heat the pans on a stove. Stay at least one meter (3 ft) away from the materials while they are heating.
4. After several minutes, you should be able to see which matter has or has not begun to decompose. Then **ask the adult** to turn off the stove.

Which substances decomposed? Some substances may have given off a gas when heated. What could the gas have been? Which substances turned black? Which substances do you think contained carbon?

2.2 Starch: A Test

Things YOU will Need:

- an adult
- eyedropper
- tincture of iodine
- saucers
- water
- teaspoon
- cornstarch
- toothpick

Chlorophyll absorbs the red and blue light that provides the energy plants need to carry on photosynthesis. Photosynthesis is a complicated chemical process in which plants convert carbon dioxide and water to oxygen and sugar. When excess sugar is produced during photosynthesis, it is stored as starch. You can carry out a test that will identify starch. In Experiment 2.3, you will use the test to see if starch is present in a leaf exposed to light.

1. **Under adult supervision**, prepare a dilute iodine solution. **Be careful handling iodine. It is a poison.** Use an eyedropper to place 100 drops of water in a saucer. Then add 10 drops of tincture of iodine to the water. The iodine solution will be used to test for starch. Rinse the eyedropper thoroughly with water.
2. Place a quarter teaspoon of cornstarch in another saucer. Add a few drops of water and stir with a toothpick.
3. To test for starch, add one or two drops of the iodine solution to the cornstarch and water mixture. What color appears when the iodine and cornstarch react? You have just seen a positive test for starch.

2.3 Photosynthesis, Leaves, and Stored Food: An Experiment

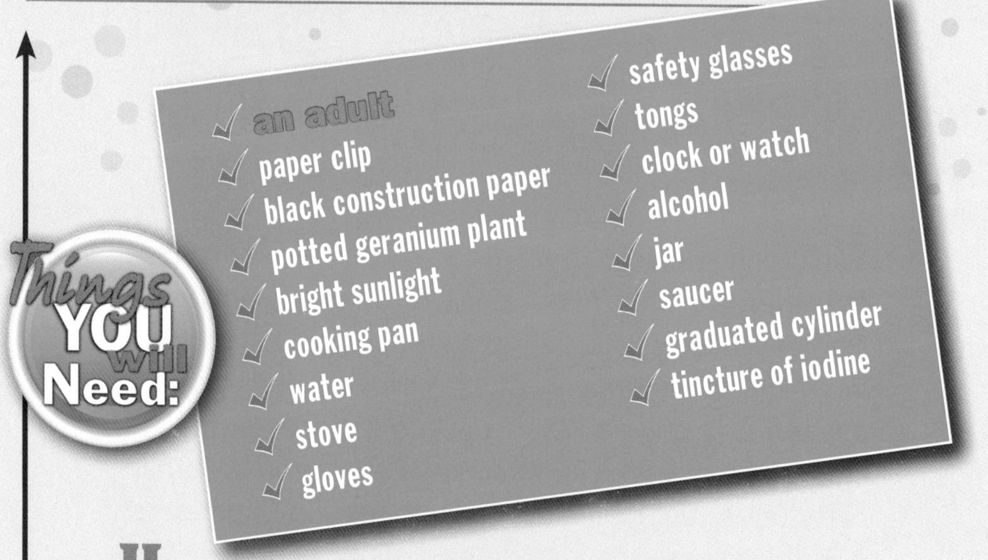

How could you test to see if green plants store food in their leaves? Form a hypothesis. Then do this experiment on a bright sunny day.

1. Place a potted geranium plant in the dark for 24 hours.
2. Use a paper clip to carefully attach a small folded piece of black construction paper to a large leaf on the geranium plant. The paper should cover both sides of part of the leaf as shown in Figure 8.
3. Put the plant in bright sunlight.
4. After four or five hours, remove the leaf from the plant and carefully unclip the paper.
5. Fill a cooking pan about one-quarter full with water. **Ask an adult** to bring the water to a boil.

Figure 8

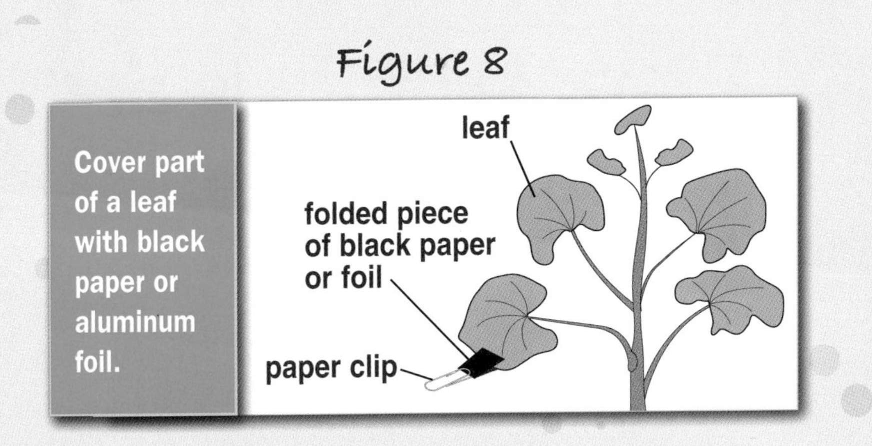

6. **Put on gloves and safety glasses.** Then, **under adult supervision,** use tongs to hold the leaf's stem and immerse the leaf into the boiling water for about one minute. The heat will break the walls of the leaf's cells.
7. Remove the leaf and turn off the stove because you will be using alcohol, which is flammable.
8. Partially fill a jar with alcohol and place the leaf inside. Leave it overnight. The next morning you will find that the alcohol has a green color due to the chlorophyll that has been extracted from the leaf.
9. **Under adult supervision**, mix 5 mL of water with 5 mL of tincture of iodine in a saucer. **Remember: iodine is poisonous. Handle it with care!**
10. Remove the leaf from the jar and rinse it in warm water. Then spread it out and place it in the iodine-water mixture in the saucer. Watch the leaf turn color as the iodine reacts with the starch to form a dark blue-black color.

Is any one area of the leaf much lighter than the rest? Can you identify that region? In which part of the leaf did photosynthesis take place? In which area of the leaf did photosynthesis not take place? How can you tell? What evidence do you have to show that light is required for photosynthesis?

2.4 Photosynthesis and Carbon Dioxide: An Author Experiment

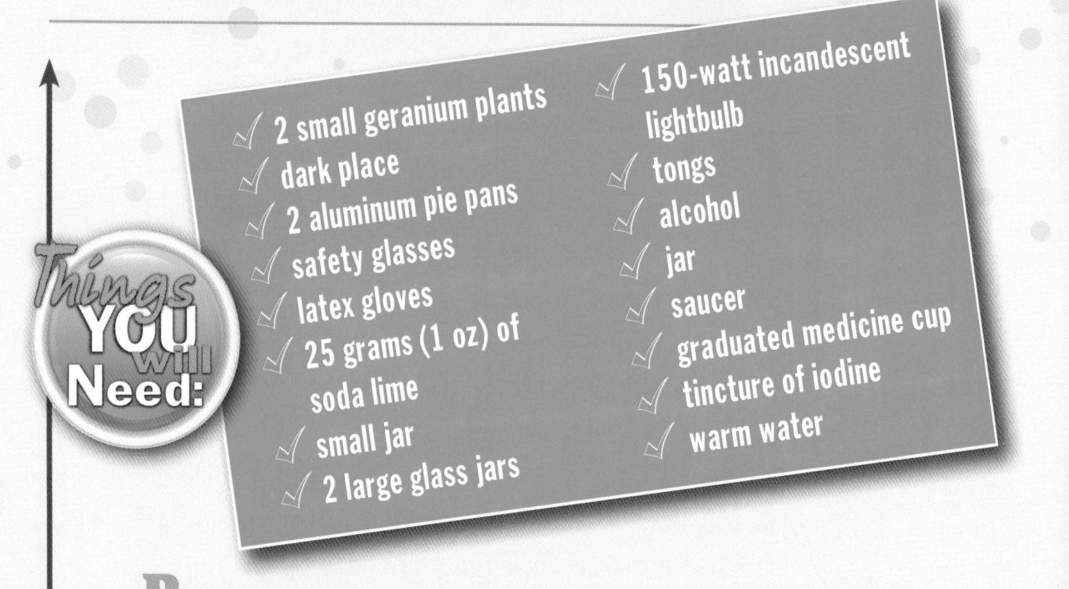

Based on what you have read, you would probably hypothesize that plants need carbon dioxide to produce food by photosynthesis. To test a consequence of that hypothesis, the author carried out an experiment. It is one that you might also do **under the close supervision of a science teacher**.

1. Two small geranium plants were placed in darkness for 48 hours. This gave the plants time to use up any stored food.

2. Each plant was placed on an aluminum pie pan, as shown in Figure 9. **Wearing safety glasses and latex gloves**, the author put about 25 grams (1 ounce) of soda lime in a small jar. **He was careful because soda lime**

is corrosive and can burn skin and eyes. Soda lime absorbs carbon dioxide from air.

3. He placed the jar of soda lime next to one plant as shown. The second plant served as a control.
4. He then covered both plants with large glass jars.
5. A 150-watt lightbulb was placed between the two plants and left on for 24 hours.
6. The light was then turned off and the jars were removed. One leaf was removed from each plant.
7. The two leaves were tested to see if they contained starch using the same method you used in Experiment 3.5. What do you think were the results of the test for each leaf?

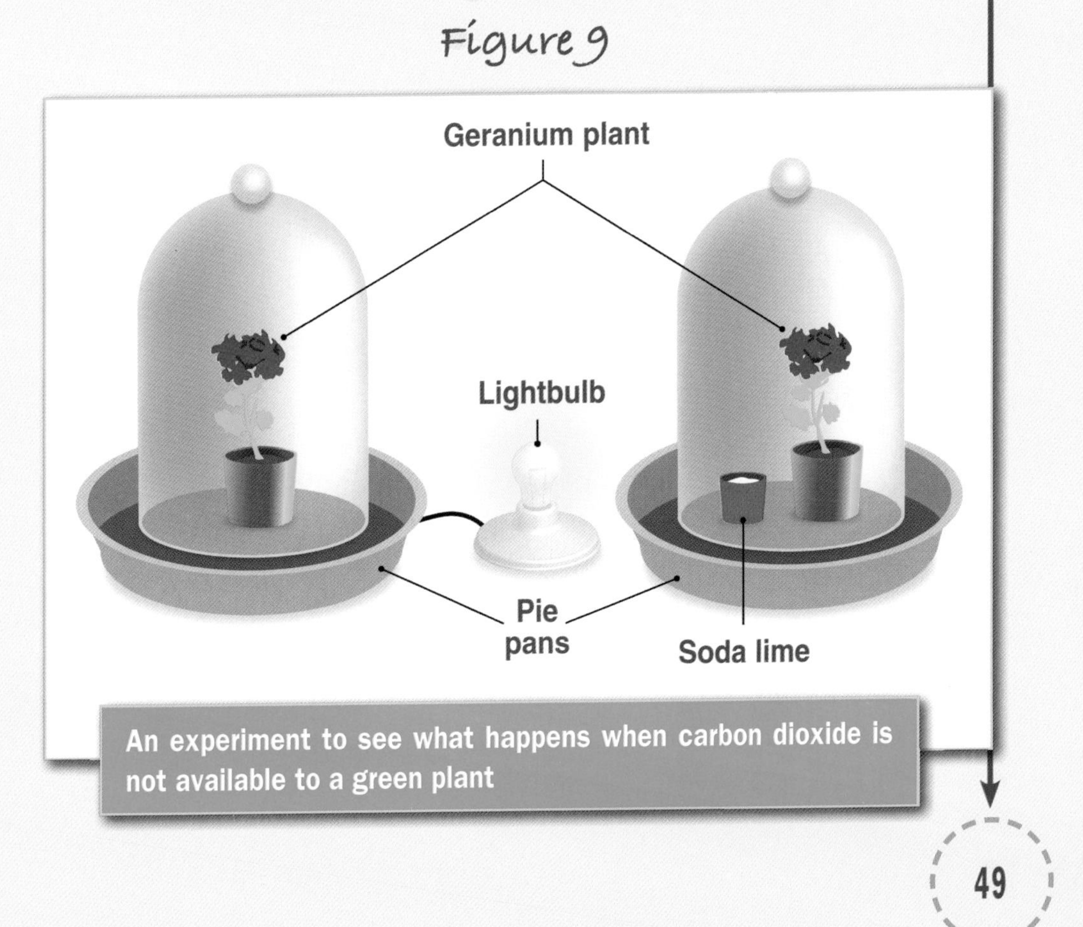

An experiment to see what happens when carbon dioxide is not available to a green plant

2.5 Photosynthesis and Carbon Dioxide:
A Demonstration

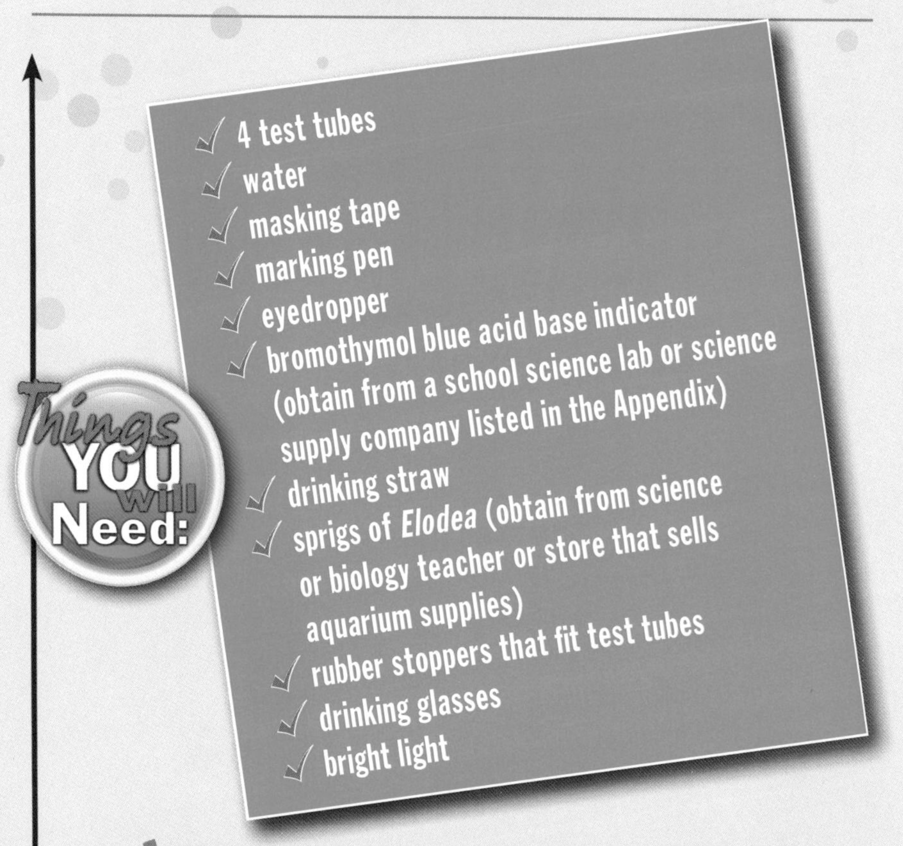

As you know, green plants combine carbon dioxide and water using light energy to produce food and oxygen. The food may be stored or used by the plant as an energy source.

Plants, like animals, carry on respiration. The food reacts with oxygen in a series of chemical reactions. These reactions release energy and produce carbon dioxide and water—the same chemicals used to make food during photosynthesis. Keep this information in mind as you do this demonstration.

As you know, carbon dioxide dissolves in water to form carbonic acid (H_2CO_3).

1. Fill four test tubes halfway with water. Place a small piece of masking tape on each tube and label them 1, 2, 3, and 4.
2. Add 1.0 mL (20 drops) of bromothymol blue to each tube. (Bromothymol blue is an acid-base indicator. It appears blue in bases, such as ammonia, and yellow in acids, such as vinegar.)
3. Using a straw, gently blow air from your lungs into tubes 1 and 2. Continue to blow until no further change occurs. Why do you think the solutions turn from blue to yellow?
4. Place sprigs of *Elodea* in tubes 1 and 3. (Elodea is a water plant commonly found in ponds. You may be able to get *Elodea* from your science or biology teacher. Or you can purchase it from a store that sells aquarium supplies.)
5. Seal the openings of all four test tubes with rubber stoppers.
6. Place the tubes in water-filled drinking glasses near a bright light source. The tubes should not be so close to the light that the water becomes hot. After several hours, record any changes you see. Continue to watch the tubes for an entire day. What changes occur?

What is the purpose of each of the four tubes in this investigation? What do the changes in each tube indicate?

What do you think would happen in each test tube if the tubes were placed in darkness instead of light?

7. Test your predictions by repeating the experiment with the plants in darkness.

2.6 Photosynthesis and Grass in Light and Darkness: An Experiment

You have seen that plants need light to carry on photosynthesis. But how does light affect chlorophyll? Will plants make chlorophyll in darkness?

Form a hypothesis. Then do this experiment.

1. With permission, place a board on some green grass near the edge of a field. Place a stone on the board to keep it in place.
2. Look under the board every few days until you can make a conclusion based on the evidence.

   What did you conclude? Why?
3. Remove the board and stone when the experiment is finished.

Idea for a Science Fair Project

Using grass seeds and soil, design and carry out an experiment to test the hypothesis that light is needed for plants to produce chlorophyll.

2.7 How Plants Adapt to Receive Maximum Light: An Experiment

Plants produce the food that makes most animal life possible. Most of the food is made in the plants' leaf cells. Herbivorous animals, such as rabbits, cows, and goats, obtain all their food from plants. Carnivorous animals, such as lions and tigers, eat the flesh of other animals. Although carnivorous animals do not eat plants, most of the animals they eat rely on plants for *their* food. Omnivorous animals, such as many humans, eat both plants and animals. In one way or another, all animals depend on plants for their food. All foods used to nourish living organisms (except for a few species of bacteria) are ultimately the product of plants or cyanobacteria. Plants produce their food in their chlorophyll-rich leaves, and they have developed a way to receive as much sunlight as possible.

Form a hypothesis to explain how you think they do it. Then do this experiment.

1. Place a potted plant near a south-facing window where the sun shines in most of the day. The plant's leaves

should either face in all directions or predominantly face the darker side of the room.

2. Keep the soil in the pot damp, but not wet.
3. Watch the plant carefully over several weeks.

What happens to the leaves? Do they turn toward the light? What does this tell you about one way green plants have adapted to their environment?

4. Once you have seen how the leaves respond to light, turn the plant 180 degrees.

How long does it take before the leaves reorient?

Phototropism

The tendency of plants to turn toward light is called phototropism. Scientists have discovered that a plant hormone causes phototropism. Light shining on one side of a plant's stem causes many of these hormone molecules to move to cells on the darker side of the stem. Once there, the hormone causes those cells to grow longer, which makes the leaf turn toward the light.

The Oxygen Cycle

In learning about the carbon cycle, you may have noticed that oxygen also goes through a cycle closely tied to the carbon cycle. During respiration, animals take in oxygen and release carbon dioxide. In that part of the oxygen cycle, oxygen is removed from the air. However, during photosynthesis, green plants take in carbon dioxide and produce oxygen. The oxygen reenters the atmosphere, keeping its concentration in air at a constant 21 percent.

Carbon Dioxide: The Most Abundant Greenhouse Gas

Environmentally, carbon dioxide is essential to living things. As you have seen in Chapter 2, carbon dioxide plays a key role in the process of photosynthesis. Without carbon dioxide, plants would be unable to manufacture food and life could not exist.

As a greenhouse gas, carbon dioxide reflects some heat back to Earth. If all the heat radiated by Earth were to escape, the planet would be too cold for life. However, the increasing amount of carbon dioxide in Earth's atmosphere is reflecting too much heat back to Earth. It is causing global warming.

In this chapter, you will learn more about this ambiguous gas. You will learn how to test for its presence and examine some of its properties.

3.1 Carbon Dioxide:
A Chemical Test

Things YOU will Need:

- limewater (Borrow some from school science department or order it from one of the science supply companies listed in the Appendix.)
- medicine cup
- drinking straw

You know that humans exhale carbon dioxide. To show that this is true, you can test your exhaled air for the presence of carbon dioxide. The test is based on the fact that limewater turns cloudy when carbon dioxide is added to it. Limewater is a solution of calcium hydroxide ($Ca(OH)_2$). It reacts with carbon dioxide to form calcium carbonate ($CaCO_3$), a white, insoluble solid. The chemical equation below summarizes the reaction.

$$Ca(OH)_2 + CO_2 \rightarrow CaCO_3 + H_2O$$

1. Pour a small amount of limewater into a medicine cup.
2. Using a drinking straw, gently blow into the limewater. What happens?

3.2 Two Properties of Carbon Dioxide:
An Experiment

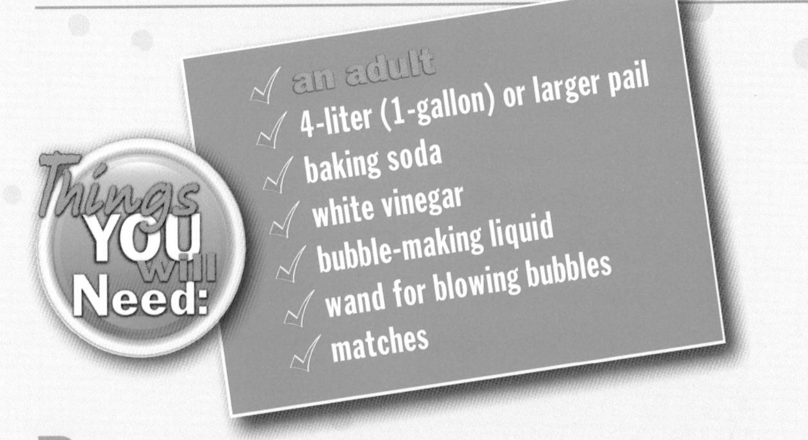

Do you think carbon dioxide is more or less dense than air? Do you think carbon dioxide will support combustion? That is, do you think things like wood will burn in carbon dioxide? Form hypotheses in response to these questions. Then do this experiment.

As you probably know, a less dense substance, such as wood, will float on a more dense substance, such as water. In this experiment, you will test to see if air-filled bubbles will float on carbon dioxide. You can make a carbon dioxide atmosphere in a 4-liter (1-gallon) pail by adding vinegar to baking soda. The chemical name for baking soda is sodium bicarbonate ($NaHCO_3$). It reacts with vinegar, a solution of acetic acid ($C_2O_2H_4$), to form carbon dioxide, sodium acetate ($NaC_2O_2H_3$), and water (H_2O). The reaction is summarized by the chemical equation below.

$$NaHCO_3 + C_2O_2H_4 \rightarrow CO_2 + NaC_2O_2H_3 + H_2O$$

1. Cover the bottom of the pail with baking soda. Add one cup of vinegar to the baking soda. The bursting bubbles of carbon dioxide will quickly create a carbon dioxide atmosphere in the bottom of the pail.
2. Dip a bubble wand into some bubble-making solution and make some large air-filled bubbles. Allow one or two bubbles to fall into the pail. You may have to move the pail so that it lies under falling bubbles.

Do air-filled bubbles float on carbon dioxide? What do you conclude about the density of carbon dioxide? Is it greater or less than the density of air?

3. Next, **ask an adult** to lower a lighted match into the carbon dioxide atmosphere. What happens to the flame? Does carbon dioxide support combustion?

Were your hypotheses correct?

This firefighter is using carbon dioxide to extinguish a fire.

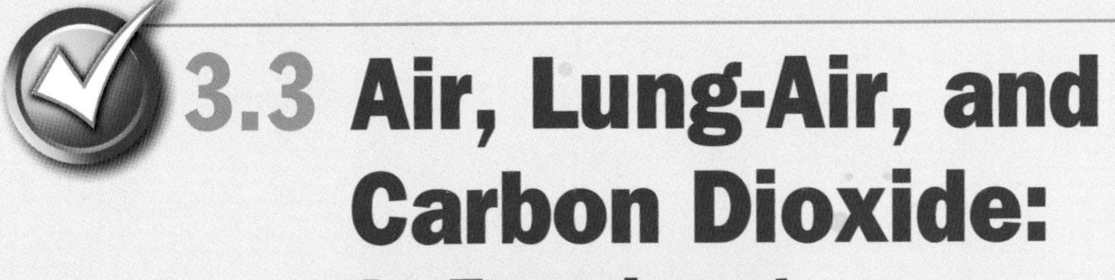

3.3 Air, Lung-Air, and Carbon Dioxide: An Experiment

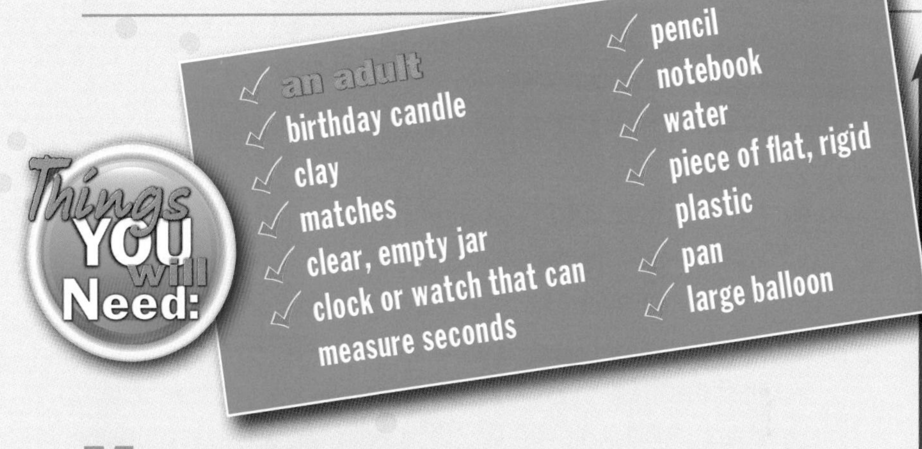

Many people think that a burning candle will go out because it has used up all the oxygen available. But early scientists performed experiments that proved this wrong.

The scientists put a mouse and a candle in a sealed jar. They ignited the candle using a lens to focus sunlight on the candle's wick. The candle burned and went out. But the mouse continued to breathe the gas remaining in the jar. The experiment showed that enough oxygen for life remained inside the jar.

Many people think that we exhale pure carbon dioxide from our lungs. What do you think?

Form a hypothesis. Then do this experiment.

One way to compare the carbon dioxide content of exhaled air with ordinary air is to compare the time that a candle will burn in a volume of air and in the same volume of air from your lungs. You can make these measurements quite easily.

1. Support a birthday candle with a small lump of clay.
2. **Under adult supervision**, light the candle.
3. After it is burning smoothly, invert an empty jar. Place it over the candle as shown in Figure 10a. Use a clock or a watch that can measure seconds to determine the time the candle burns in the fixed volume of air. Record the time.
4. Next, **under adult supervision**, fill the same jar with water, cover its mouth with a piece of plastic, and invert it in a pan of water. Then remove the cover.
5. Take a deep breath. Use a length of rubber tubing or a flexible straw to blow air from your lungs into the water-filled jar (Figure 10b). Your lung-air will replace the water in the jar, providing you with a container of exhaled lung-air.
6. **Under adult supervision**, relight the candle.
7. When the candle is burning smoothly, remove the jar of lung-air from the water and place it over the burning candle. Does the candle go out immediately? If not, record the time that the candle burns.

   Use the times you have recorded to estimate the carbon dioxide content of air with that of lung-air.

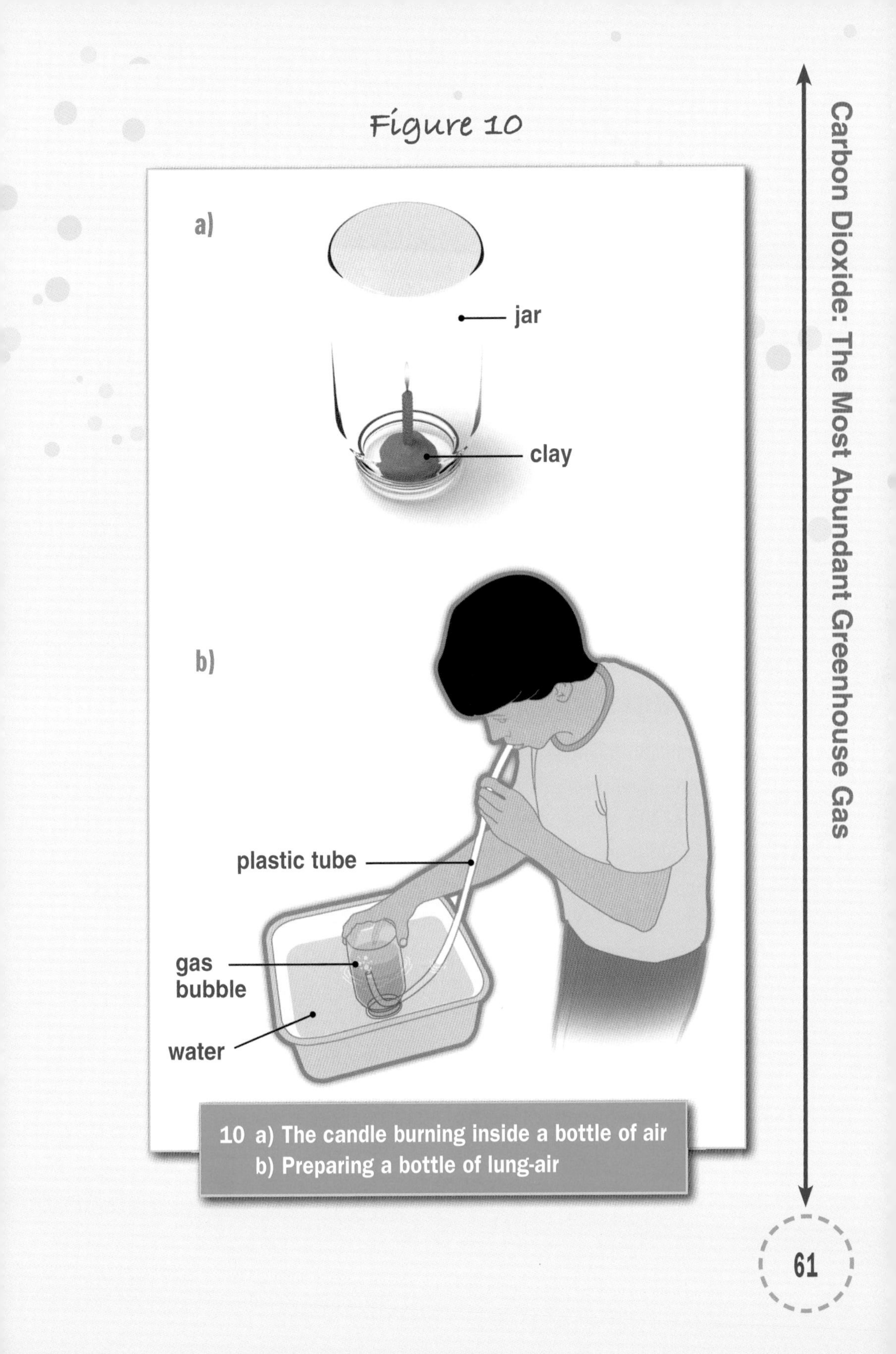

10 a) The candle burning inside a bottle of air
b) Preparing a bottle of lung-air

Ideas for Science Fair Projects

- Repeat Experiment 3.3, but this time hold the air in your lungs for about 30 seconds before using it to fill the jar. Does keeping the air in your lungs increase its carbon dioxide concentration? How can you tell?
- Ordinary air is about 21 percent oxygen and 0.04 percent carbon dioxide. The concentration of nitrogen in both inhaled and exhaled air is 78 percent. Design and carry out an experiment to determine the percentage of oxygen and carbon dioxide in exhaled air.

Measuring Gas Densities

It is difficult to measure the density of a gas, such as carbon dioxide, in air. In the first place, gases have little mass because most of the space they occupy is empty. Gas molecules are about ten times farther apart in all three directions than are the molecules in a solid or a liquid. Therefore, gas densities are only about 1/1,000 the densities of solids and liquids. Secondly, as Archimedes demonstrated, objects in air are buoyed upward by the weight of the air they displace. Since the density of air at room temperature is about 1.20 g/L, a liter of gas weighed in air will appear to have a mass that is 1.20 grams less than its actual mass. If a gas is less dense than air, it will appear to have negative weight; it will, like a helium balloon, ascend in air.

To weigh gases, chemists use a vacuum to pump all the air out of a vessel they have weighed. Then they let a gas flow into the empty vessel through a valve. After closing the valve and disconnecting the source of the gas, they reweigh the vessel. The increase in mass is the mass of the gas. Knowing the volume of the vessel and the mass of the gas they can calculate the gas's density. The density of some common gases determined in this way is found in Table 1.

As this photograph of a hot air balloon shows, hot air is less dense than colder air.

Table 1:
Density, in Grams Per Liter (g/L), of Six Common Gases at Room Temperature (20°C, 68°F) and Air Pressure at Sea Level.

Oxygen (O_2)	1.33	Helium (He)	0.166
Air	1.20	Hydrogen (H_2)	0.083
Carbon dioxide	1.84	Nitrogen (N_2)	1.16

3.4 Preparation and Density of Carbon Dioxide: A Measurement

Things YOU will Need:

- graduated cylinder or metric measuring cup
- cold water
- round balloon
- a small, clear bottle or flask that has a narrow neck (an aspirin bottle that held 250 pills will do)
- twisty tie
- balance that can weigh to ± 0.01 gram
- seltzer tablets
- a partner
- cloth measuring tape
- calculator (optional)
- pencil
- notebook

In Experiment 3.2, you prepared carbon dioxide by adding vinegar to baking soda. A less vigorous and easier to control reaction uses seltzer tablets and water. Seltzer tablets contain both citric acid ($C_6H_8O_7$) and sodium bicarbonate ($NaHCO_3$). Like vinegar, citric acid will react with sodium bicarbonate to produce carbon dioxide.

1. Pour about 50 mL of cold water into a small, clear bottle or flask that has a narrow neck.
2. Obtain a round balloon. Weigh the balloon and a twisty tie on a balance that can measure mass to the nearest hundredth (0.01) of a gram.
3. Break two seltzer tablets in half.
4. Drop the tablets into the water. Then pull the neck of the balloon over the mouth of the bottle as shown in Figure 11. The gas will collect in the balloon.

   Look at the gas being produced. Is it colored or colorless?

Figure 11

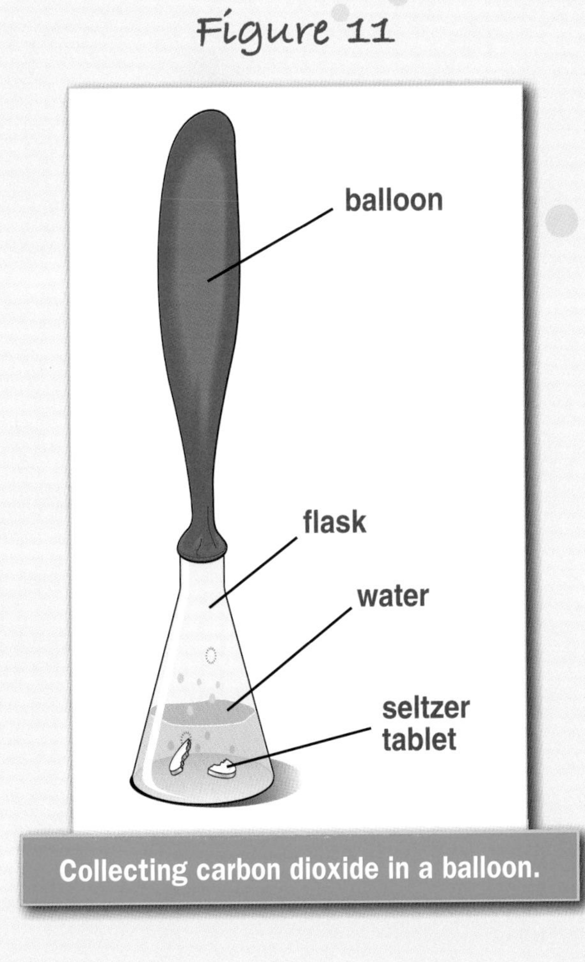

Collecting carbon dioxide in a balloon.

5. Wait until gas is no longer being produced or the fizzing has nearly stopped. Then grasp the neck of the balloon so no gas can escape and remove the balloon from the bottle. Ask a partner to help you use a twisty tie to seal the neck of the balloon so no gas can escape.
6. Use a cloth metric measuring tape to take several measurements of the balloon's circumference. Then weigh the balloon and enclosed gas to the nearest hundredth of a gram.
7. Calculate the average circumference of the balloon. Assume the gas-filled balloon is a sphere. Then calculate its diameter. Remember, circumference equals pi (π) x diameter (D) or $C = \pi D$, so $D = C/\pi$.
8. Assuming the thickness of the balloon is negligible, calculate the volume of gas in the balloon. Remember: the volume of a sphere equals $4/3\ \pi r^3$, where r is the balloon's radius (D/2). For example, suppose the average circumference of the balloon was 36 cm. Its diameter would be:

$$\mathbf{D = C/\pi = 36/\pi = 11.5\ cm.}$$

Its volume would be:

$$\mathbf{V = 4/3\ \pi r^3 = 4/3\pi\ (5.75\ cm)^3 = 4/3\pi\ (190) = 796\ cm^3}$$
$$\mathbf{or\ 0.796\ L}$$

because there are 1,000 cm^3 in a liter (L).

9. Calculate the density of the carbon dioxide. Remember, density (d) equals mass/volume and the gas is buoyed upward by the mass of the air displaced.

For example, suppose the gas and balloon weighed 2.00 g and the empty balloon and twisty tie weighed 1.50 g. The additional mass caused by the gas in the balloon would be 0.50 g because 2.00 g – 1.50 g = 0.50 g.

However, as Archimedes discovered long ago, the gas-filled balloon is buoyed upward by the mass of the air it displaces. Since the density of air at room temperature is 1.20 g/1,000 mL, the buoyant effect on the balloon would be:

1.20 g x 796/1,000 = 0.96 g.

Therefore, without the buoyant effect, the gas would weigh 0.96 g + 0.50 g = 1.46 g. Its density would be:

1.46 g/0.796 L = 1.83 g/L.

Ideas for Science Fair Projects

- Do an experiment to show that air weighed in air appears to be weightless.
- Do an experiment to show that water weighed in water appears to be weightless.
- Table 1 gives the densities of gases at a particular temperature and pressure. Do experiments to show how temperature and pressure affect the volume of a gas.

The Water, Nitrogen, and Phosphorus Cycles

Earth's water is constantly moving. Raindrops fall, rivers flow, and ocean waves break on beaches. But there is also movement we don't see—the motion of water molecules. Earth's water moves in a cycle as shown in Figure 12. Water evaporates (changes from liquid to gas) from lakes, rivers, puddles, plants, and the ground. The gaseous water becomes part of the air. Then it condenses and falls back to Earth as rain. The cycle continues as the water again evaporates and reenters the air. The annual quantities of water that move in this never ending-cycle are also shown in Figure 12.

Figure 12

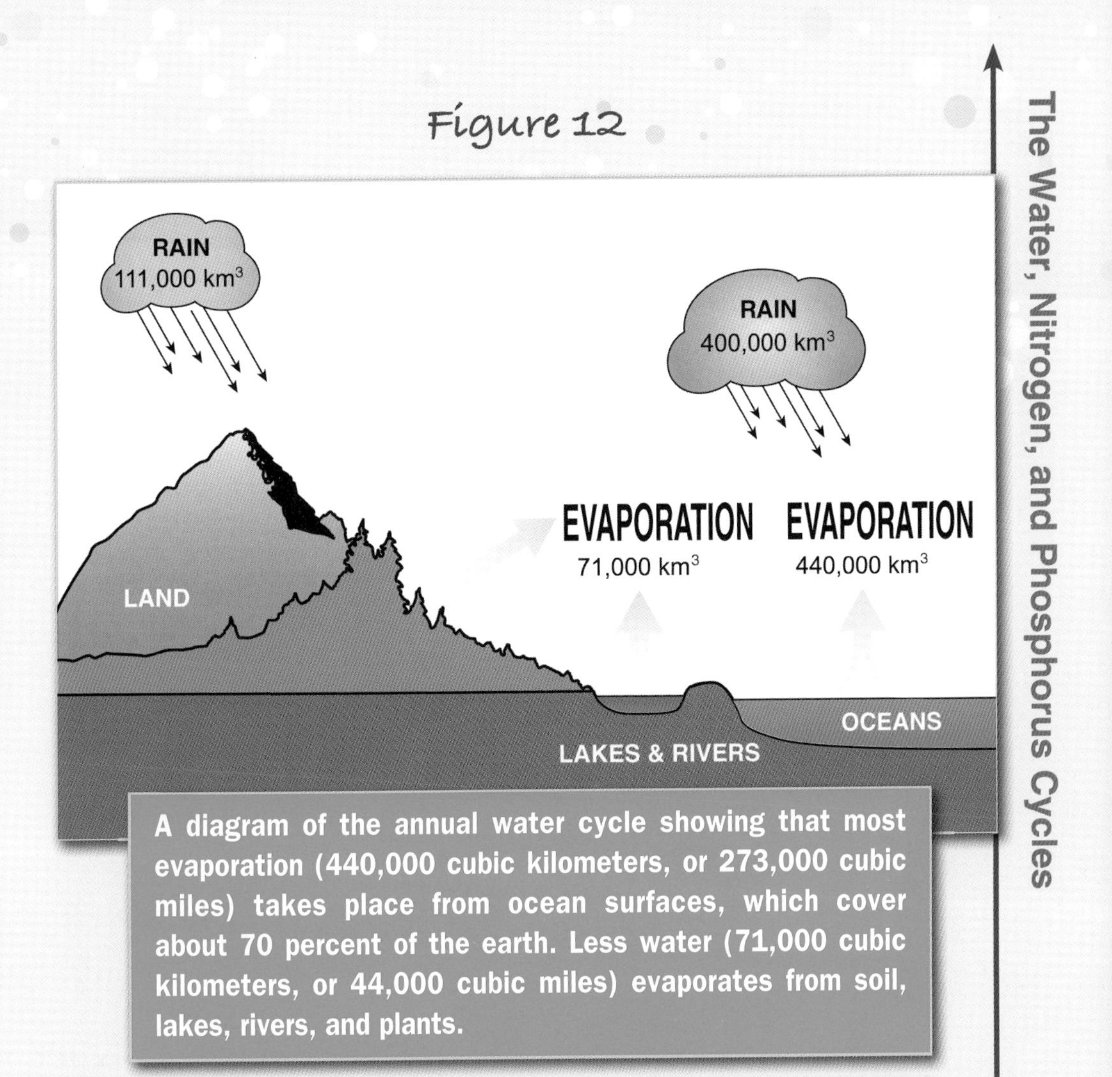

A diagram of the annual water cycle showing that most evaporation (440,000 cubic kilometers, or 273,000 cubic miles) takes place from ocean surfaces, which cover about 70 percent of the earth. Less water (71,000 cubic kilometers, or 44,000 cubic miles) evaporates from soil, lakes, rivers, and plants.

Earth's total amount of water changes very little. Comets carry small amounts of snow into the atmosphere. That snow melts and vaporizes. Each comet carries about 20 to 40 tons (4,800 to 9,600 gallons) of water. Comets have added about 2,700 cubic kilometers (650 cubic mi) of water to Earth over the last 10,000 years—a tiny percentage (0.0002%) of Earth's total water. A few gaseous water molecules reach a velocity of 11.2 kilometers per second (7 mi/s) and escape to outer space. Anything moving at this speed (known as the escape velocity), can escape Earth's gravity. Space probes sent to explore other planets and beyond must reach speeds equal to or greater than escape velocity.

Earth's water has a total volume of 1,370,000,000 cubic kilometers (328,000,000 cubic mi). However, 97 percent of that liquid is unfit to drink because it is salty ocean water. An additional 37,500,000 cubic kilometers (9,000,000 cubic miles), which accounts for 95 percent of the world's fresh water, exists as ice near the earth's poles. Only about one-third of one percent of Earth's water is available for use by humans and other Earth-dwelling plants and animals.

Water flows along rivers and ocean currents, but the motion of most of the world's water is vertical, upward into the air as invisible water vapor and downward as rain.

4.1 The Water Cycle: A Model

Things YOU will Need:

- water
- ruler
- plastic pan
- sheet of clear glass or plastic
- small aluminum pan
- ice cubes
- bright sunlight or heat lamp

You can make a model to represent the water cycle.

1. In a plastic pan that is about 5 centimeters (2 in) deep, pour water to a depth of about one centimeter (0.4 in). The water represents all open water, including oceans, lakes, and rivers. Place a wood block at one end of the pan to represent land.
2. Cover the pan with a sheet of clear glass or plastic, which will represent Earth's atmosphere. If you use plastic wrap, tape it to the sides of the pan.
3. Fill a small aluminum pan with ice cubes. Put it on one side of the plastic or glass cover. It represents the cold clouds in the air above the water.
4. Place the pans in bright sunlight or under a heat lamp (Figure 13).
5. After a few minutes, you will see water droplets condensing on the lower side of the cold clear sheet. You may even be able to detect smaller drops joining to form larger ones that fall back like rain onto the "ground" below. If not, create some "thunder" by tapping on the pan.

Figure 13

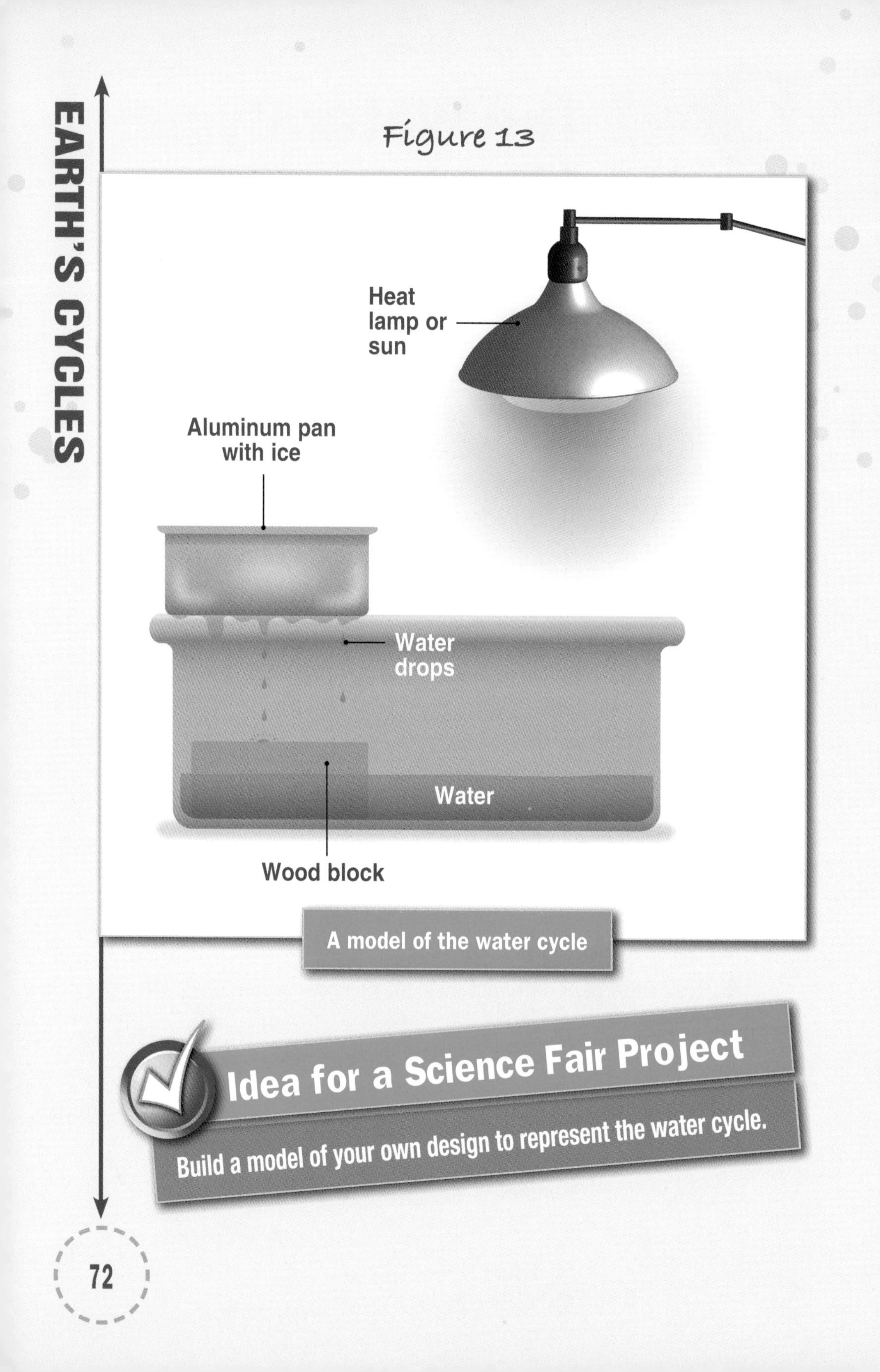

A model of the water cycle

Idea for a Science Fair Project

Build a model of your own design to represent the water cycle.

4.2 Evaporation of Ocean Water: An Experiment

Things YOU will Need:

- an adult
- teaspoon
- kosher salt
- cup
- warm water
- spoon
- wide pan
- saucer
- cooking pan
- cup (metal if possible)
- aluminum foil
- ice cubes
- stove
- sink

About 85 percent of the water that evaporates into the air comes from the oceans. As you know, ocean water is salty. The ocean is a huge salt solution. Do you think that the water that evaporates from the oceans is salty?

Form a hypothesis. Then do this experiment.

1. Add one teaspoonful of kosher salt to one cup of warm water and stir until the salt dissolves.
2. Pour the salt solution into a wide pan. Place the pan in a warm, secure place where the water can evaporate over several days.
3. When all the water has evaporated, examine the pan. What do you see? What evidence do you have that evaporated ocean water is not salty?

Figure 14

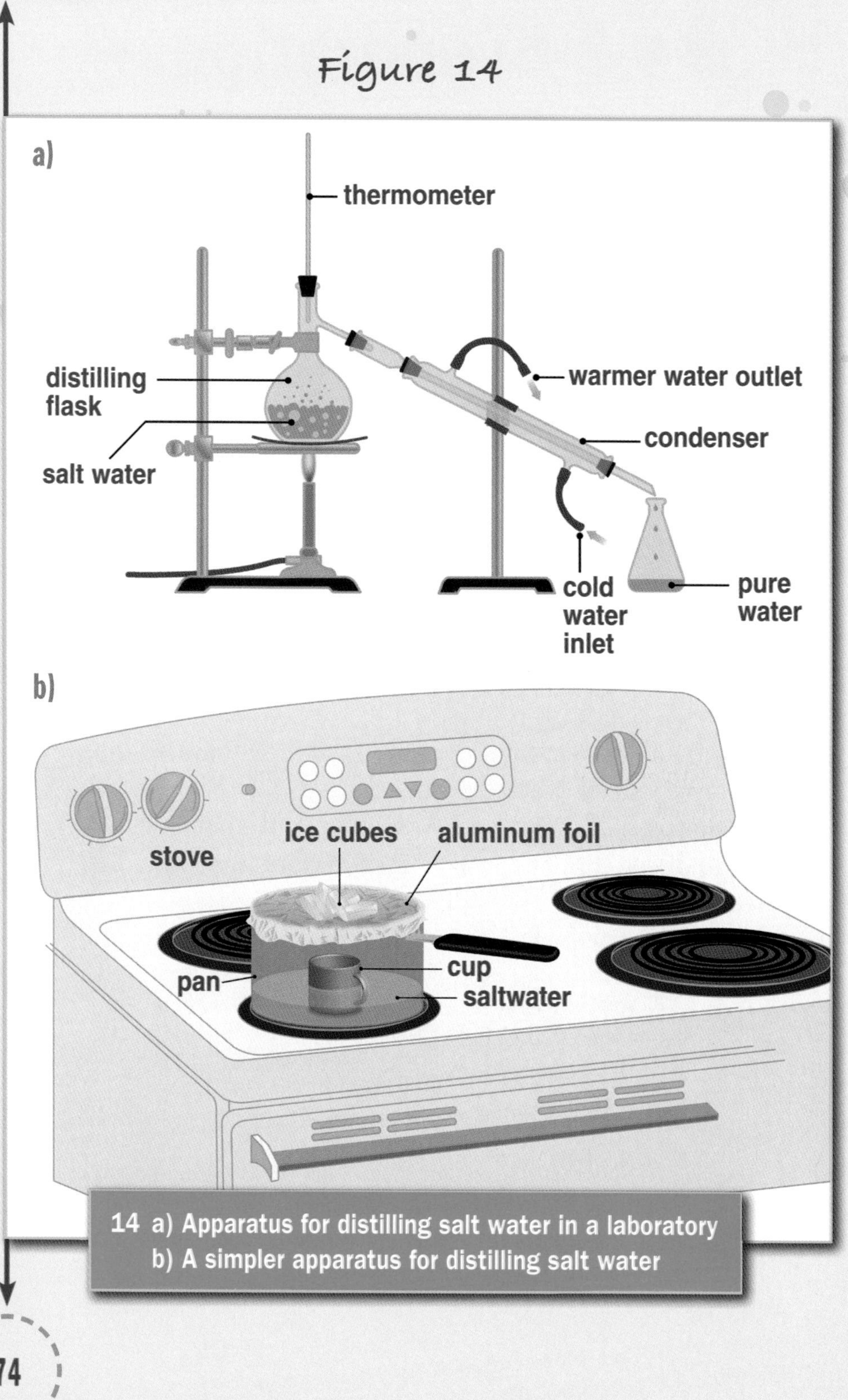

14 a) Apparatus for distilling salt water in a laboratory
b) A simpler apparatus for distilling salt water

Chemists use an apparatus shown in Figure 14a to distill (evaporate) water. The salt solution in the flask is heated and it boils. The water vapor rises and enters the condenser, where it cools, condenses back to a liquid, and collects in the flask at the lower end of the condenser. The process is called distillation. You can distill using materials available in your kitchen.

4. Add one teaspoon of kosher salt to one cup of warm water and stir until the salt dissolves. Pour the salt solution into a cooking pan.

5. Wash your hands. Then dip a finger into the salt solution. Bring that finger to your tongue. You should be able to taste the salt.

6. Place an empty cup in the center of the pan.

7. Securely cover the cooking pan with a sheet of aluminum foil as shown in Figure 14b. Add a few ice cubes to the center of the aluminum foil.

8. **Ask an adult** to place the pan on a stove and heat the salt-water solution. Let the water boil gently until most of the ice has melted. If you have a metal cup in the pan, you may be able to hear water dripping into the cup.

9. Have **the adult** place the pan in a sink and carefully remove the aluminum foil, melted ice, and the cup.

10. Wash your hands again. When the cup has cooled, use a finger to taste the liquid that collected in the cup. Is it salty?

What liquid do you think is in the cup? What do you think was the purpose of the ice on the aluminum foil cover? How is the process you just did similar to the process shown in Figure 14a? How is it different?

Idea for a Science Fair Project

What is fractional distillation? How can it be used to separate two liquids, such as isopropyl alcohol and water? **Under the supervision of a science teacher**, use fractional distillation to separate a 1:1 mixture of isopropyl alcohol and water. How can you identify the two liquids after separating them?

Desalination

Obtaining fresh water that one can drink is a growing problem in much of the world. Distilling ocean water is one way to obtain drinkable water, but it is a very expensive process.

More efficient desalination plants have been built in Singapore and Tampa Bay, Florida. These plants use pressure to force water molecules through membranes that allow the passage of water but not salt.

Future desalination plants will probably use filters made of carbon nanotubes, which offer more efficient filtering at less cost. However, even plants using nanotube filters will require significant quantities of electrical energy. As you can see, the path to a greener world is not an easy one.

Are We Running Out of Water?

Water shortages are a worldwide problem. Water for irrigating crops accounts for 70 percent of fresh water consumption. Much of that water is pumped from wells drilled into aquifers (saturated groundwater). Unfortunately, water is being removed from aquifers faster than it is being replaced by rainfall. To reach the water in shrinking aquifers, wells have to be drilled deeper. The deeper wells require more energy to pump the water to the surface.

In the United States, the Ogallala Aquifer was formed several million years ago by melting glaciers. It lies under most of Nebraska, as well as parts of South Dakota, Wyoming, Colorado, Kansas, Oklahoma, New Mexico, and Texas. Many farmers in these states pump water from the Ogallala to irrigate their crops and provide water for their cattle. However, the aquifer is only being replenished at about one-tenth the rate at which it is being pumped. As a result, this aquifer will soon be dry. Some farmers have been forced out of business. Others are switching to crops that require less water.

Similar problems with aquifers exist elsewhere. China's wheat crop has fallen by eight percent since it peaked in 1997. Its rice crop has diminished by four percent over the past decade as well. In India, millions of wells have gone dry. Many of India's power companies cannot meet the energy demands of the many pumps used to bring up water from aquifers where water tables are one kilometer (0.6 mi) below the surface.

The same is true of the world's rivers. River water is removed to irrigate crops, provide for household and industry use, including the generation of electricity, and by evaporation. By the time many rivers reach their ultimate destinations (oceans, lakes, or other rivers), little if any water is left. The Colorado River, for example, is dry by the time it reaches the ocean.

Restoring freshwater aquifers and rivers will require more efficient ways to use water. Farmers can water crops using underground drip irrigation rather than conventional flooding or spraying. Farms can shift to growing crops that require less water. For example, growing wheat rather than rice, which requires lots of water, will reduce water requirements. Power plants can reduce water use by switching to dry cooling rather than water cooling. And more electric power can be generated by sources that do not require water, such as solar and wind. In our homes, we can install efficient appliances that use less water.

We can reduce the threat of floods from runoff water, conserve soil, and reduce atmospheric carbon dioxide by planting trees. Trees have roots that hold soil and its water in place. And, like all green plants, trees absorb carbon dioxide, thereby combating global warming.

Conserving Water

We can all do our part to conserve water, a resource we cannot live without. The average person in the United States uses about 250 liters (65 gal) of water each day. By carefully conserving water using the ideas listed below, you and your family should be able to reduce that usage by 30 percent.

In the Bathroom

- Install low-flow faucets and showerheads.
- Replace old toilets with low-flush toilets, which use only 6 liters (1.6 gal) per flush. Or put sealed stone-filled or

sand-filled bottles in toilet tanks to take up space normally occupied by water. Be sure enough water remains to adequately flush the toilet.

- Repair leaky faucets and toilets.
- Flush toilets only when necessary.
- Take short showers instead of baths.
- Don't let water run while brushing your teeth or soaping your hands or face.
- Never use a toilet to flush away toxic or hazardous waste materials. They can seep into groundwater and contaminate drinking water.

In the Kitchen, Laundry, and Basement

- Run the dishwasher only when it is full. Use the minimum number of washes or rinses and let dishes air dry. Use detergents that do not contain phosphates.
- Do not run water continuously when washing dishes in the sink.
- When replacing a washing machine, buy a front-loading machine. They use less water and energy.
- Do not use a garbage disposal in your sink. It requires lots of water and can add grease and solids to a sewage or septic system.
- Do not put hazardous wastes in the trash or pour them down your drains. Most towns have special days when hazardous wastes are collected and properly disposed of.
- Avoid using laundry detergents with brighteners. Brightener compounds can kill fish and other aquatic life. They also biodegrade slowly.

Outdoors and in the Garage

- Control erosion due to water by planting trees and shrubs.
- If you have a lawn, cut grass no shorter than three inches. This will promote healthy turf, which holds rainwater, filters sediments and chemicals, and requires less watering.

- Do not use fertilizers or insecticides on your lawn. They pollute ground water.
- Water lawns and gardens only when necessary. Water early in the morning or after sunset. Otherwise, much of the water evaporates.
- Use a broom, not a hose, to clean driveways and walks.
- Wash your car only when necessary. Use a bucket and hose with a shutoff nozzle.
- Take old, used automobile products, such as antifreeze, wax, and polish to a hazardous waste site. Most landfills or transfer stations will accept used motor oil for recycling. These items should never be poured down a drain or emptied on the ground. They can make ground water unsafe to drink.

Do Your Part to Make People Aware of the Need to Conserve Water

Be an advocate for water conservation and other green issues. Write letters or e-mail your town council members, mayor, congressional leaders, and senators. Prepare posters that support water conservation. Speak out about water conservation and making America green in your classes and with your family and friends.

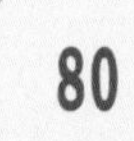

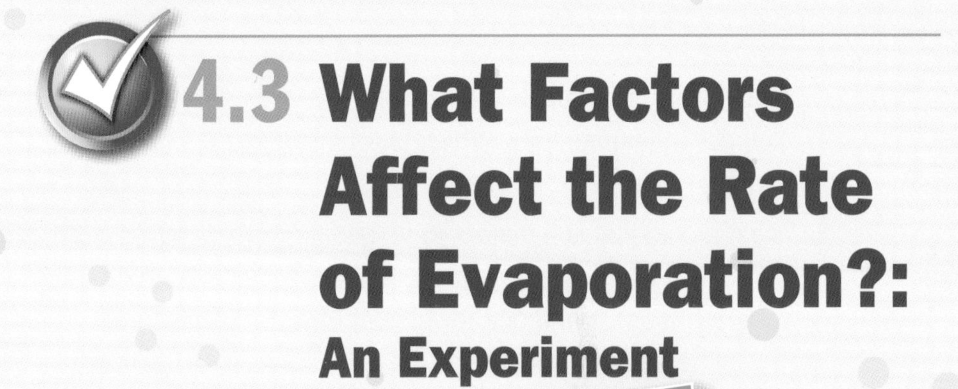

4.3 What Factors Affect the Rate of Evaporation?: An Experiment

What factors do you think affect the rate of evaporation?

Form a hypothesis. Then do this experiment.

You may have noticed that in humid weather perspiration tends to remain on your skin. So one of the factors that affect the rate of evaporation is the amount of moisture already in the air (humidity). To investigate other factors affecting evaporation, you can do this experiment.

1. Soak two identical paper towels in water. Use clothespins to hang one towel in a place that is warm and dry. Hang the other towel in a place that is cool and dry. Which towel dries faster? How is evaporation affected by temperature?
2. Soak two identical paper towels in water. Fold one towel again and again until it is a small rectangle. Use

clothespins to hang both towels side by side on a clothesline (Figure 15a). Which towel dries faster? How is evaporation affected by surface area?

3. Hang a cord that is 2 meters (6 ft) long horizontally across part of a basement or a garage. Soak two identical paper towels in water. Hang one towel near one end of the cord. Hang the second towel near the other end of the cord. Use a fan to blow air across one of the towels (Figure 15b). Leave the other in still air. How does moving air (wind) affect evaporation?

Figure 15

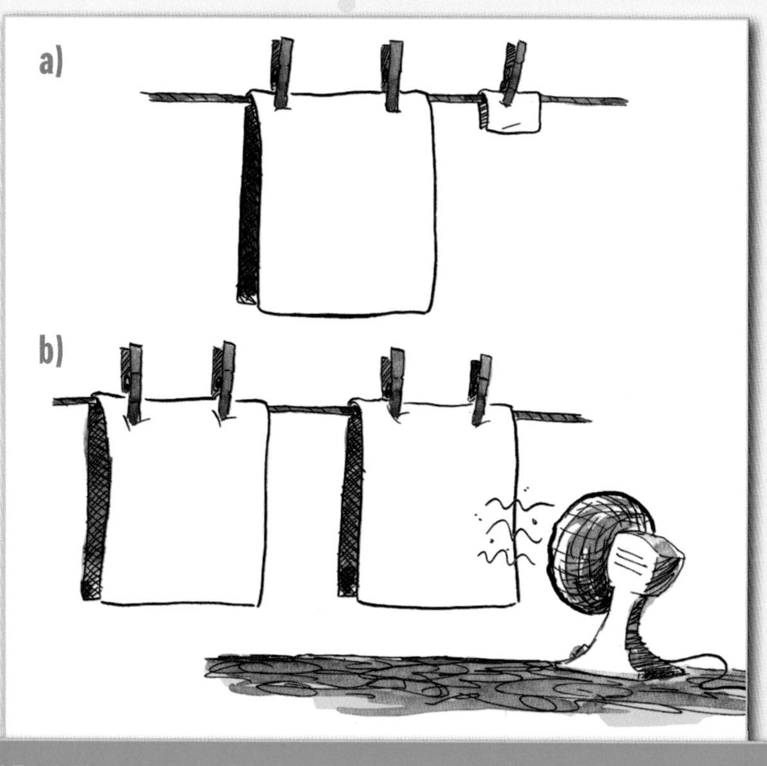

15 a) How does surface area affect the rate of evaporation?
b) How does a wind (moving air) affect the rate of evaporation?

Idea for a Science Fair Project

Design and carry out an experiment to show that moving air has no effect on air temperature.

The Nitrogen Cycle

Nitrogen is an element that makes up 78 percent of Earth's atmosphere. It is combined with other elements in all protein molecules. Protein is found in all living organisms and is one of the three basic foods along with fats and carbohydrates.

In the nitrogen cycle (Figure 16), nitrogen moves from the atmosphere to the soil to living tissues and back to the air. Tiny organisms, known as nitrogen-fixing bacteria, are able to convert nitrogen gas to compounds (nitrates) that are soluble in moist soil. Some of these bacteria live in the soil. Others live on the roots of legume plants, such as clover, alfalfa, beans, and peas.

The nitrates in soil are absorbed by plants through their roots and used to make protein and other organic compounds essential to life. These nitrogen-containing compounds become part of the living cells of animals that eat the plants. The nitrogen compounds are transferred to other animals through the food chain.

Bacteria and fungi called decomposers break down animal and plant waste and remains. Decomposers change the waste into nitrogen-containing compounds

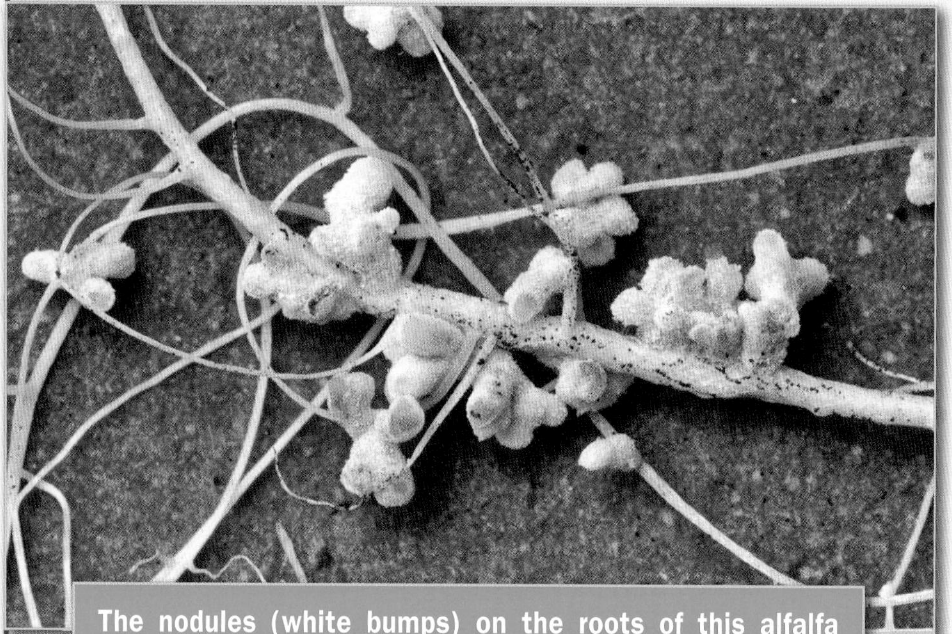

The nodules (white bumps) on the roots of this alfalfa plant contain nitrogen-fixing bacteria. The bacteria convert nitrogen gas into a form that the plant can use.

that are acted on by nitrifying bacteria. The nitrifying bacteria change the nitrogen compounds into nitrates, forming a subcycle within the nitrogen cycle.

Some of the nitrates in soil are acted on by denitrifying bacteria that convert the nitrates back to nitrogen gas that reenters the atmosphere. Farmers try to prevent their fields from becoming soaked with water because denitrifying bacteria are abundant in wet ground and remove nitrates from the soil.

The nitrogen cycle, like all of Earth's cycles, can be influenced by human actions. Many farmers add chemical fertilizers, such as ammonium nitrate (NH_4NO_3), to their fields to ensure that their crops have a good supply of nitrates. Nitrogen compounds in the soil become part of the cells of the plants that

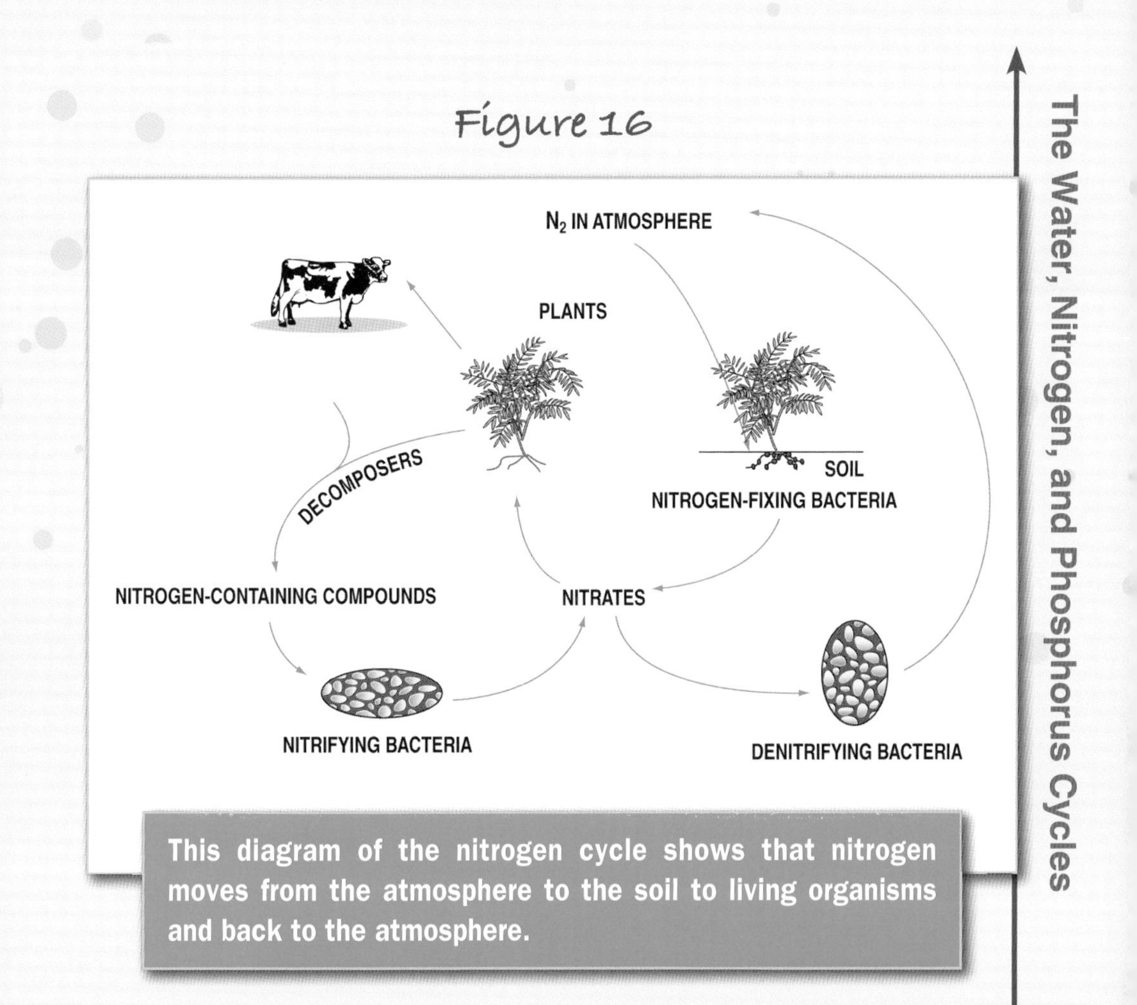

This diagram of the nitrogen cycle shows that nitrogen moves from the atmosphere to the soil to living organisms and back to the atmosphere.

are harvested. As a result, nitrogen is removed from the soil. The nitrogen is often replaced by adding more chemical fertilizer at the beginning of the next growing season. Many farmers and homeowners use much more fertilizer than is needed. Rain often carries these nitrates from the farm fields and lawns to nearby rivers, lakes, and ponds where it can stimulate the growth of algae. Often, the algae become so abundant that they blanket the water with a green cover. This cover prevents light from reaching plants that grow below the surface causing them to die. As bacteria work to decompose the dead water plants they respire, reducing the water's oxygen content. The water soon becomes deficient in oxygen, and unfit for certain fish and other animals.

Burning fossil fuels adds nitrogen oxides to the air. These nitrogen compounds become part of the nitrogen cycle as well as air pollutants. For example, nitrous oxide (N_2O) is a more potent greenhouse gas than carbon dioxide. Fortunately, it is far less abundant in the atmosphere than carbon dioxide.

To counter the harmful effects on the nitrogen cycle, we need to burn less fossil fuels. This means replacing power plants that burn fossil fuels with renewable energy sources—solar, wind, geothermal, tidal—that do not add nitrogen compounds to the air. Driving fuel-efficient automobiles will also help. Earth-friendly farming can also reduce the damaging effects of nitrate fertilizers.

Organic Farming

Organic farmers do not use synthetic nitrate fertilizers. Instead, they spread organic matter, such as compost or manure, on their fields. This method adds nutrients to the soil and improves conditions for crops and soil-forming organisms, such as earthworms. These farmers may plant winter crops, such as rye or wheat, to help the soil hold its nitrogen. Such crops carry on photosynthesis, which absorbs carbon dioxide from the atmosphere, keeping more carbon in the plants instead of the air.

They may also grow more grasses and less corn. Corn plants have shallow roots that do not hold soil well. As a result, water runoff from cornfields carries soil and nitrates into streams, lakes, and ponds promoting algae growth.

Corn is a very popular crop in the United States. Many farmers are paid by the U.S. government to grow corn. It is used to make ingredients, such as high fructose corn syrup, which are then added to many processed foods. Corn is also widely used to feed cattle, chickens, and hogs. We could reduce the nitrate problem by eating fewer processed food products that contain corn-based ingredients and less meat. Or we could eat only beef from cattle that are range-fed on year-round grass plants.

4.4 Isolating Gaseous Nitrogen:
A Demonstration

Things YOU will Need:

- an adult
- fine steel wool that does not contain soap
- jar
- white vinegar
- water
- shallow, plastic container
- food coloring
- plastic gloves
- 3 tall, narrow jars
- pencil
- paper
- shallow box and rubber band (optional)
- marking pen or rubber bands
- ruler
- small glass or plastic plate
- matches
- thin strip of wood such as a thin wooden coffee stirrer

Nitrogen gas can be prepared by the distillation of liquid air. The nitrogen can be separated from the oxygen. Nitrogen boils at –195.6°C (–320.1°F). This temperature is lower than the boiling point of oxygen, which is –183.8°C (–298.8°F), the other major component of air. Consequently, nitrogen begins to boil before oxygen as liquid air is slowly warmed from a temperature close to absolute zero (–273.15°C or –459.7°F). It can also be prepared by heating ammonium nitrite (NH_4NO_2), which decomposes into nitrogen and water as shown below.

$$NH_4NO_2 \rightarrow N_2 + 2H_2O$$

In this demonstration, you will prepare nitrogen by removing oxygen from air.

1. Soak part of a pad of fine steel wool that does not contain soap overnight in a jar containing equal volumes of vinegar and water. The liquid mixture will remove any oil that may cover the steel, which is primarily iron.
2. Add water to a shallow, plastic container to a depth of about 2 cm (1 in). Add several drops of food coloring to make the water more visible.
3. Put on plastic gloves. Pull a few strands of steel wool from the pad that was soaked in the vinegar solution. Roll them into a small loosely packed ball. Make two such balls from the steel wool. They should be slightly larger in diameter than the two tall narrow jars that will be used in the experiment. Olive jars will work well.
4. Place a steel wool ball into each of two tall jars. Use a pencil to push a steel wool ball to the bottom of each jar. A third jar will serve as a control. Push a small wad of paper to the bottom of the third jar.
5. Turn the jars upside down. Place them side by side in the shallow pan of colored water as shown in Figure 17a. If the tubes are "tippy," use a rubber band to fasten them to a support, such as a shallow box, so that they remain firmly upright.

Figure 17a

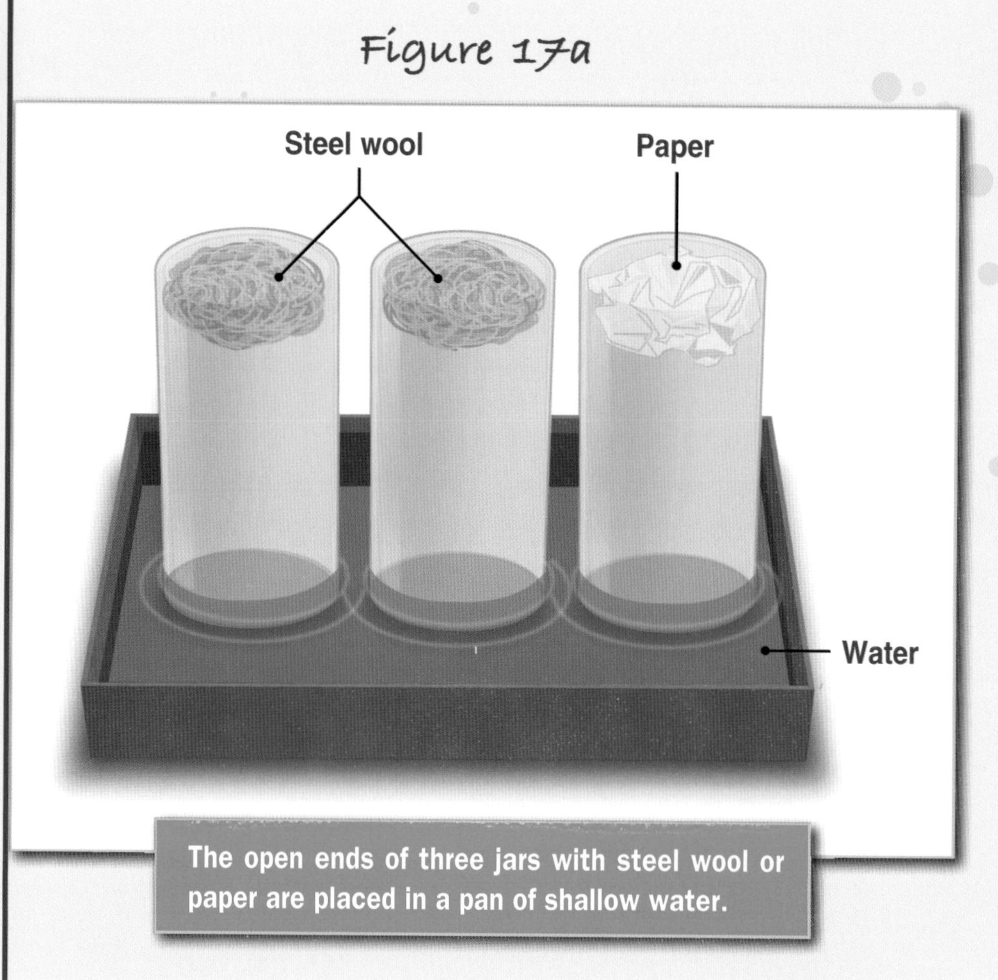

The open ends of three jars with steel wool or paper are placed in a pan of shallow water.

6. Leave the jars for 24 hours. In which tubes did the water rise? Use a marking pen or rubber bands to mark the water level in each tube. Leave them for several more hours. Does the water continue to rise? If it does, wait until it stops rising. Then mark the new levels.
7. Look closely at the steel wool in the jars. Has it rusted? Has the water risen in the tube with a paper ball?

The oxygen in two of the jars reacted with the iron in the steel wool to form iron oxide (rust). The water has risen in these jars to replace the oxygen.

8. Use a ruler to measure the water level in each jar. What is the ratio of the height of the water level to the total length of the jar? What percentage of air is oxygen according to your experiment? For example, suppose the water rose 3 cm in a tube that is 15 cm long. The ratio height of water to height of tube is:

$$\frac{3.0 \text{ cm}}{15.0 \text{ cm}} = \frac{1.0}{5.0} = 0.20 = 20\%.$$

How do your measurements of the percentage of oxygen in air compare with 21 percent, which is the accepted percentage of oxygen in air?

9. If all the oxygen was removed from the air, the gas that remains is mostly (99%) nitrogen.

What are the properties of nitrogen? You can observe its properties just by looking at it in air or in the jars. Is it colored or colorless? As you may know, oxygen supports combustion; that is, things will burn in oxygen. Does nitrogen support combustion? You can find out by using the jars of nitrogen you have collected.

10. To see if nitrogen will support combustion, slide a small glass or plastic plate under the mouth of one of the jars. The plate serves as a seal covering the mouth of the jar (Figure 17b).

11. Hold the plate firmly against the jar as you lift it out of the water and invert it so the plate-covered mouth is upright as seen in Figure 17c.

12. **Ask an adult** to light a thin strip of wood, such as a thin, wooden coffee stirrer.

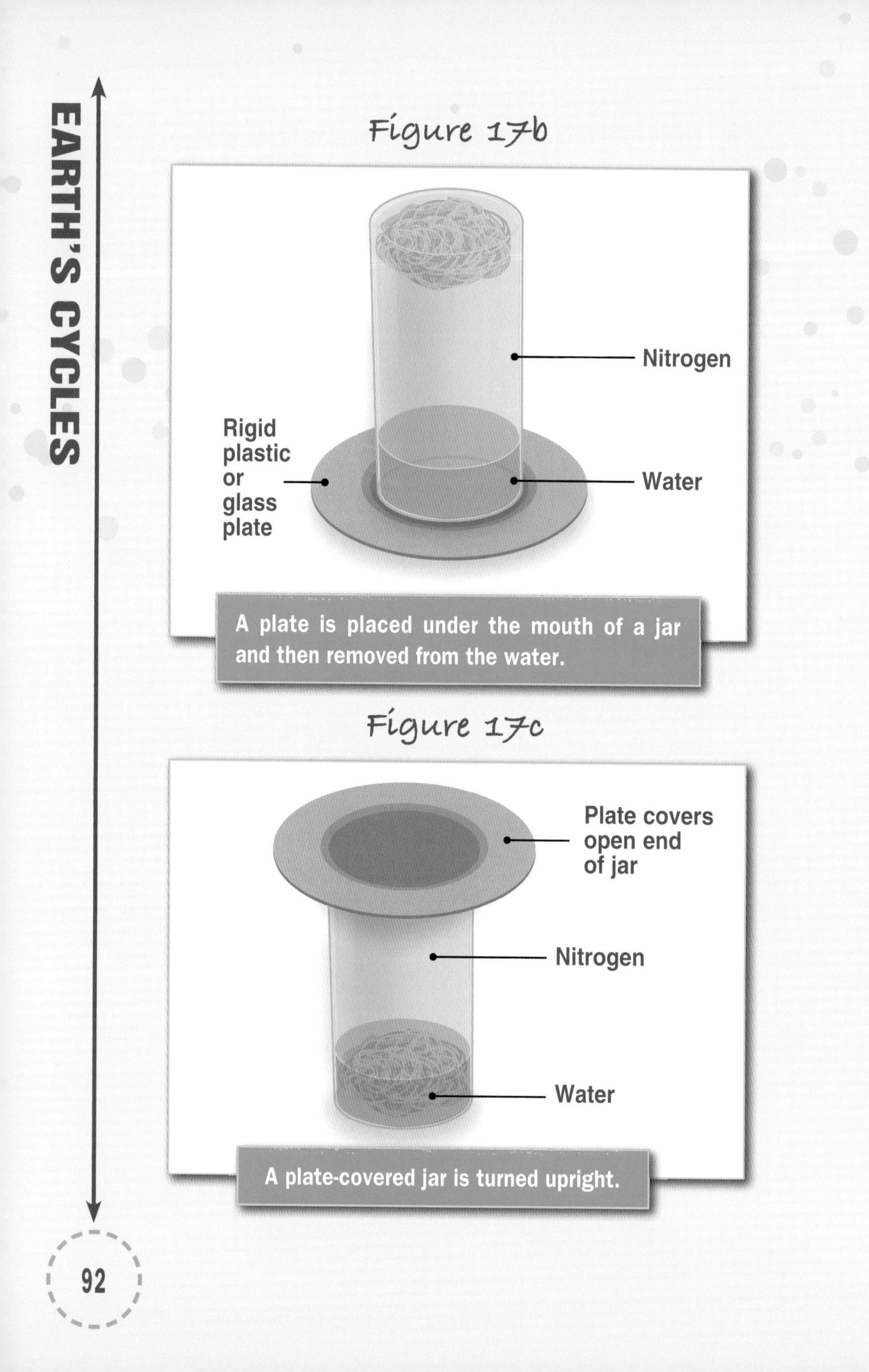

A plate is placed under the mouth of a jar and then removed from the water.

A plate-covered jar is turned upright.

13. Remove the cover and **ask the adult** to immediately put the burning splint into the jar (Figure 17d). Does nitrogen support combustion? How do nitrogen and air compare in terms of their ability to support combustion?

Ideas for Science Fair Projects

- **Show that the volume of the steel wool was negligible compared to the volume of the jar.**
- **Under adult supervision, prepare oxygen gas and test it for its ability to support combustion by using a glowing splint.**

Figure 17d

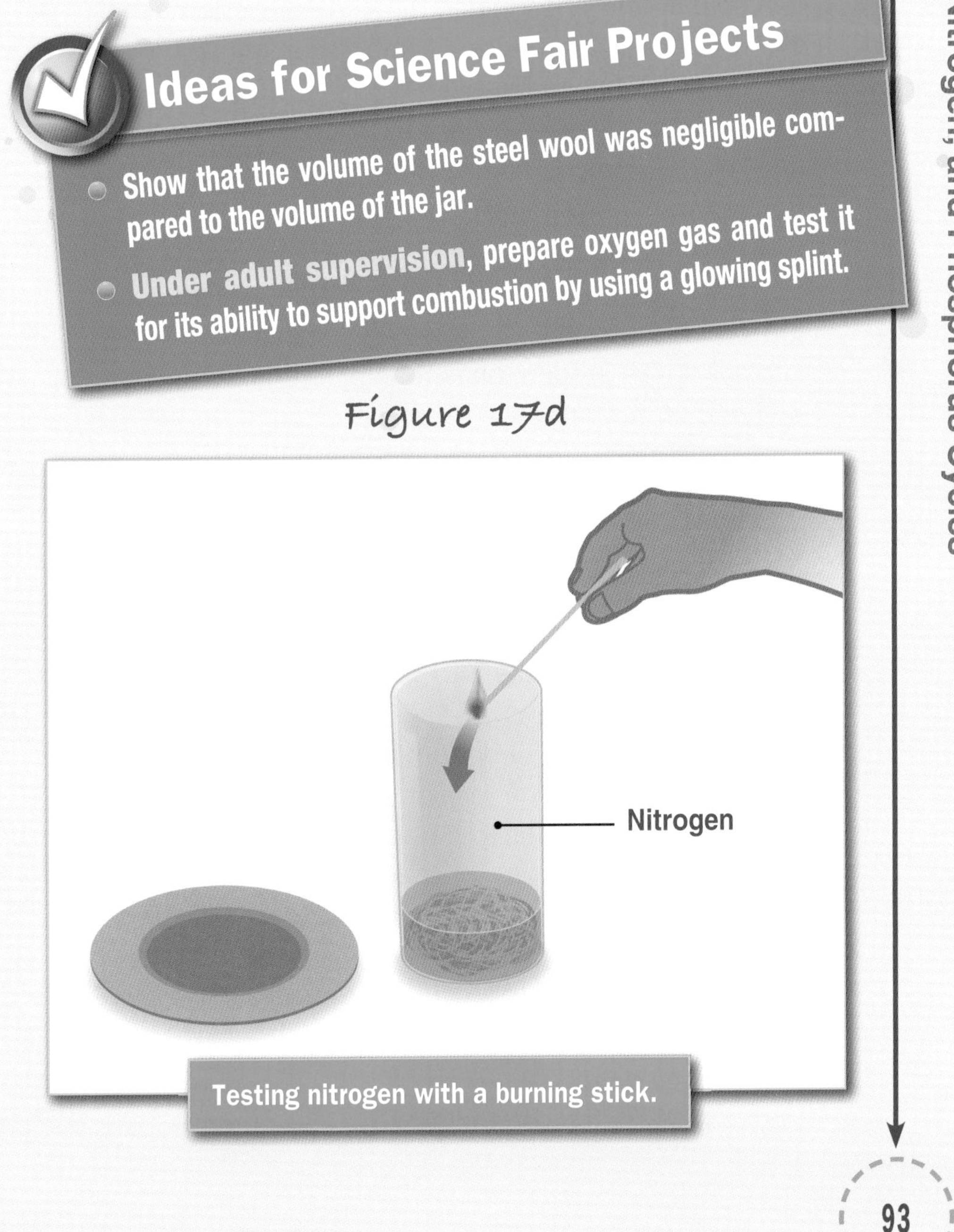

Testing nitrogen with a burning stick.

The Phosphorus Cycle

Phosphorus, like nitrogen, is an element essential for life because it is an ingredient of proteins and the DNA that contains our genes. Its most common compounds are phosphates. Its importance to animal life is evident from the fact that 60 percent of bones consist of calcium phosphate.

Phosphates in soil are absorbed by plant roots and used in making phosphorus compounds that are needed by all living cells. Animals obtain their phosphates by eating plants.

When plants and animals die, decomposers act on the organic compounds releasing phosphates back into soil. Like nitrogen, phosphates from fertilizers and detergents can speed the growth of algae in water. This growth can use up oxygen in the water causing fish and other water animals to die.

A Concern for a Greener Earth

Some phosphates wash into the oceans. Because many phosphate salts are not very soluble, they become part of the ocean floor. Slowly, over millions of years, seafloor sediments undergo geological processes and become rocks that emerge on land.

The widespread use of phosphate fertilizers has reduced the availability of this resource needed by all living things. Some scientists estimate that U.S. phosphate sources will be gone in less than a century.

The loss of phosphates to lakes, rivers, and ponds can be reduced by using agricultural methods similar to those discussed for nitrates—no-till farming, terracing, winter crops, and growing less corn.

Chapter 5

Population Cycles

To understand population cycles, you need to know the terms listed below.

- *Birth rate:* The number of live human births per year per thousand residents of a region, country, or any geographic area. In the United States, it is about 14/1,000/year.
- *Death rate:* The number of deaths per year per thousand residents of a region, country, or any geographic area. In the United States it is about 8/1,000/year.
- *Population growth rate:* The rate of increase or decrease in a population expressed as a percentage per year. Since U.S. births exceed deaths by 6/1,000/year, the U.S. population of 306,000,000 is increasing by 1,836,000 per year, or at a growth rate of 0.6 percent per year.
- *Fertility rate:* The average number of offspring a female member of a population is likely to have based on present birth rates. This varies greatly in the present human population from about 1.4 in Europe to 5.2 in Africa.

- *Replacement rate:* The number of offspring each female must have to maintain zero population growth. Because some offspring do not survive, the rate is always greater than two. For humans in developed countries, such as the United States, the rate is about 2.1; in developing countries, it is as high as 3.5.
- *Carrying capacity:* The maximum number of individuals that resources will allow without compromising (reducing living standards) the population's future inhabitants.
- *Doubling time:* The time for a population to double. The current doubling time for the world population is about 50 years.

The population of any species depends on many factors. Disease, the number of predators, competition for food, water, and space, and changes in climate all affect the population of a particular plant or animal species. A population increases when the number of births exceeds the number of deaths. It decreases when deaths exceed births. It becomes stable when birth and death rates are equal.

5.1 Population Cycle: A Model

We can make a model of a population and follow it through a number of generations. Many animal populations have a cycle similar to the one you will discover using this model.

1. Let's assume that a pair of field mice find a lush meadow unoccupied by any other mice.
2. Assume, too, that this pair of mice (the first generation) produces 10 offspring, 5 males and 5 females.

   To account for the fact that some mice die, let's assume that all parent mice in this and succeeding generations die after raising their litters (offspring). Also assume that the mice reproduce once each year.
3. In the second year, assume each of the 5 pairs of offspring in the second generation also produce 10 offspring, 5 males and 5 females. The population of mice has now grown from 10 to 50.
4. In the third year, 25 pairs of mice, 25 males and 25 females, each produce 10 offspring raising the population to 250, 125 males and 125 females.
5. During the fourth year, 125 pairs of mice each produce 10 offspring increasing the population to 1,250 mice.

6. At the beginning of the fifth year, the farmer who owns the meadow buys several cats to control the mice because they are invading his barn. The cats feast on the abundant population of mice reducing the population of mice to 250.
7. During the sixth year, 125 pairs of mice each produce 10 offspring increasing the population to 1,250 mice. However, the cats catch 1,000 mice so the mouse population remains at 250 and continues to remain at 250 until the present, which we will assume is 10 years since the first pair of mice entered the meadow.
8. Plot a graph of the population of mice in the meadow from year 0 to year 10.

Idea for a Science Fair Project

Investigate how scientists measure the population of a species in a given area. Then try to estimate the population of some species of plants or animals in an area near where you live.

Figure 18

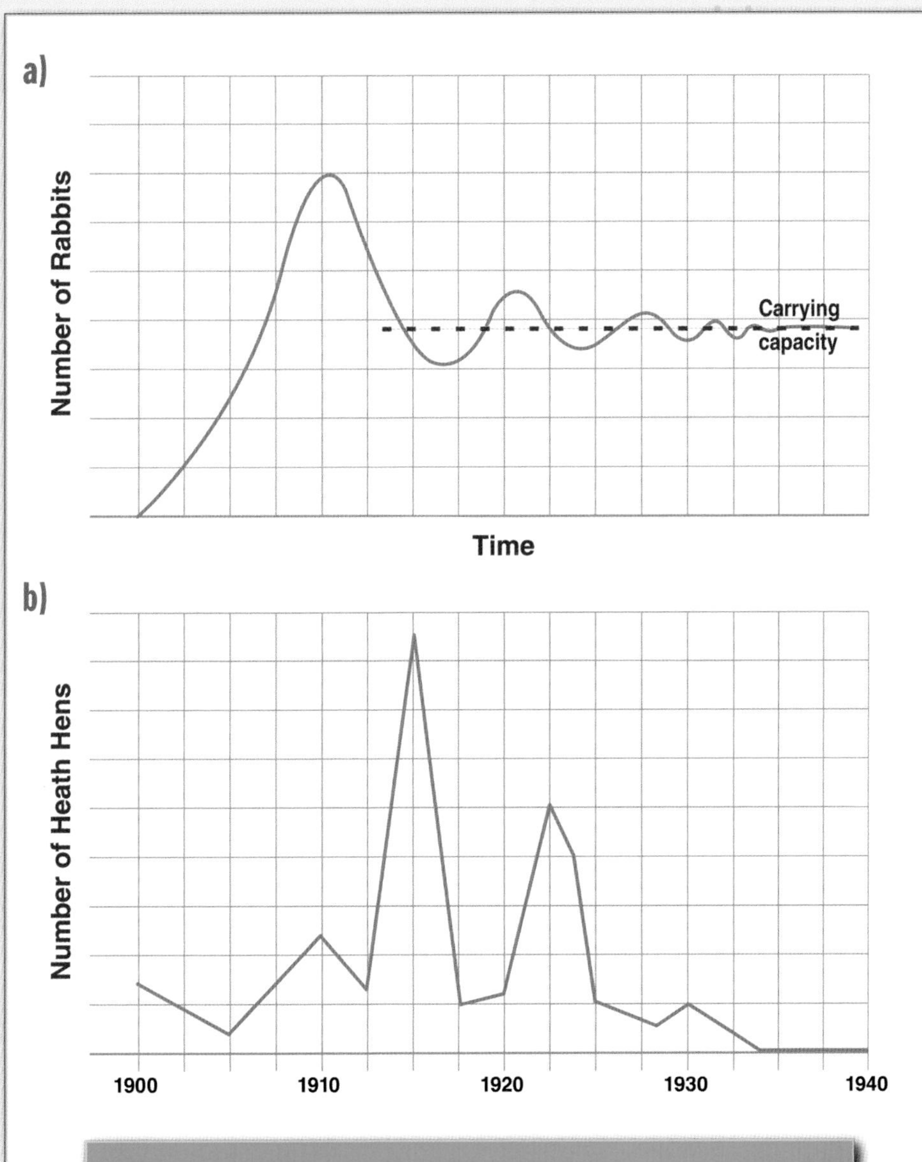

18 a) A graph showing changes in the rabbit population cycle in Australia.
b) A graph showing heath hen population cycle on Martha's Vineyard, Massachusetts.

Rabbits in Australia and Other Population Cycles

The graph you drew in Experiment 5.1 is a typical population cycle. A similar graph can be used to show what happened after Thomas Austin released 24 European rabbits on his Australian ranch. Within 16 years, the rabbits had spread across the continent. They destroyed grassland, burrowed under buildings, and became incessant pests. Eventually, their numbers exceeded their food supply, predators found ways to catch them, and a virus spread through their population. Figure 18a shows how their population increased exponentially, declined, and then fluctuated from year to year about a level known as their carrying capacity.

Sometimes, the population of a species follows one like that of the heath hen, which is shown in Figure 18b. What happened to heath hens? Make a graph showing the hypothetical population cycle of a species of dinosaurs.

You will examine the human population through time in the next analysis.

5.2 Human World Population: An Analysis

Table 2 contains figures of estimates of the world's population since 1500.

Table 2: World Population Estimates from 1500 to 2010.

Year	Population (in billions)	Year	Population (in billions)
1500	0.50	1970	3.70
1650	0.55	1974	4.00
1750	0.73	1980	4.46
1804	1.00	1990	5.30
1850	1.18	1995	5.73
1900	1.60	1999	6.00
1925	2.00	2007	6.67
1950	2.60	2009	6.80
1960	3.04	2010	6.83

1. On graph paper, plot points for a graph of world population versus time. Plot time along the horizontal axis and population along the vertical axis.
2. Draw a smooth curve through the points you have plotted to show world population growth from 1500 to 2010. Allow room to extend the graph to 2050.

What is the shape of your graph? What does it tell you?

At what point in time did the human population begin to increase dramatically?

What do you predict the world's population will be in 2050?

What was the doubling time for Earth's population from 1500 to 1804? From 1804 to 1925? From 1925 to 1974? What do you predict the next doubling time will be?

3. Make a second graph using just the data in the second column. Allow room to extend the graph to 2050. Draw a smooth curve through the points you have plotted.

What do you predict the population will be in 2050 according to this new graph? Which graph do you think gives you the best estimate for the population in 2050? Why do you think so?

What do you estimate the population will be in 2020?

Assume your estimate of the world's population in 2020 is correct. What is the difference between the population in 2020 and 2010?

4. Predict the population in 2020 by using the annual fractional increase in population. To estimate the annual fractional increase, divide the increase in world population

between 1999 and 2010 (0.83 billion) by 11 years. Divide that number by 6 billion to find the annual fractional increase in population (0.0126). Assuming the fractional increase remains constant, what will be the world's population in 2020?

5. You can use the y^x key on a calculator to make another estimate of the world's population in 2020. The fractional increase in population per year is now down to 0.011, which is an annual population increase of 1.1 percent. The population after one year will be 1.011 times greater than it was the previous year. Enter 1.011 into the calculator and press the y^x key, then press 21. That is the number of years between 1999 and 2020. Finally, press the equal sign. The number that appears is the ratio of the population in 2020 to the population in 1999. If you multiply the 1999 world population by the number on your calculator, you will have an estimate of the world's population in 2020. What do you estimate that population to be?

What you are doing when you use the y^x key is multiplying 1.011 by itself 21 times.

How does the estimate made using a calculator compare with the estimate you made using the graph? Suppose the rate at which the population is changing increases before 2020. Will your estimate then be too high or too low? How will your estimate be affected if the rate at which the population is changing decreases before 2020?

If an annual growth rate of 1.1 percent continues, how long will it take for the population to double? In what year would we expect the world's population to reach 12 billion?

Some experts estimate that the world's population will reach 9 billion some time between 2040 and 2050. What is your estimate?

As you have seen, the world's human population is growing. It may have reached or exceeded its carrying capacity, a capacity that is being reduced by global warming and the pollution of air, water, and soil. However, there is a basis for optimism because the rate is decreasing. In 1963, the world's population was growing 2.2 percent per year. Today, that rate has been halved. Population growth can be further slowed and eventually stopped by improving education and making health care available to all people.

Population and Food

An ever-growing world population can lead to a food shortage. A shortage of food means that food will cost more and many will go hungry.

There are three major factors that hamper attempts to increase the grain production needed to feed a growing world population. Those factors are loss of topsoil, a shortage of freshwater, and global warming. Ways to conserve water and improve its quality were discussed in Chapter 4.

Topsoil, which took millions of years to reach an average depth of 15 cm (6 in), is eroding. Nutrients found in topsoil are essential for plant growth. Without sufficient topsoil, grain crops will diminish and food prices will increase significantly.

Some farmers are already using methods that conserve soil. These include such things as: (1) terracing fields to reduce water erosion; (2) planting trees to shield against winds that blow soil away; (3) rotating crops; (4) practicing minimum tillage by not plowing so as to leave crop residues to enrich the soil.

Global warming is a widespread threat to food production. A temperature increase of 1°C (1.8°F) decreases grain crops by 10 percent. Some regions may become too dry to grow any crops.

We can meet this global crisis by the collective action of the world's countries. To combat global warming, we need to reduce the amount of carbon dioxide entering the atmosphere. We can do this by obtaining our energy from sources other than fossil fuels. We need to switch to renewable energy sources—wind, solar, geothermal, tidal, and possibly nuclear power—as quickly as possible.

What You Can Do to Make a Greener Earth

Conserve energy!

- Most of our energy comes from fossil fuels that produce carbon dioxide, a greenhouse gas. A few ways to conserve energy include:
- Walking, biking, and using public transportation instead of using automobiles.
- Using energy-efficient appliances in your home.
- Installing low-flow showerheads and fluorescent lighting.
- Lowering thermostats at night and when you are away.
- Installing solar panels to generate much of your own electricity from the sun.
- When cars are needed, drive automobiles that are fuel-efficient, car pool, and avoid unnecessary mileage by combining trips.

- Be sure your home is well insulated.
- Be sure window frames and sills are caulked to prevent warm air from escaping and cold air from entering your living space.
- Choose green electricity from wind, solar, hydroelectric, geothermal, tidal, wave, and nuclear sources even though the cost may be more.
- There are many other ways to conserve energy. How many can you think of?

Conserve soil!

- Make your own soil by composting food scraps and yard waste. You can use compost to make or add to a garden. Be sure your garden is on level ground, terraced, or enclosed by logs or large lumber so that soil cannot erode.
- If you have a lawn, leave grass clippings on the lawn. They serve as a natural mulch and fertilizer for the soil. Long grass clippings can be added to your compost or used as garden mulch.
- Never walk or drive on dune grass. Dune grass traps sand and holds beach soil in place.
- Do not use chemical fertilizers on lawns. It can contaminate the underlying soil and groundwater. Use organic fertilizers instead.
- Plant grass and other vegetation on sloped ground to prevent soil erosion.
- Plant trees and bushes. They hold soil in place and reduce erosion. But do not plant trees near walks, pools, or septic leach fields. Their roots can crack or raise concrete or macadam and block septic drains.

Glossary

Alpha Centauri—The next closest star to Earth after the sun. It is greater than four light years away.

aphelion—The point in the sun's orbit when it is farthest from Earth (about 152 million kilometers, or 94 million miles).

Archimedes principle—A body is buoyed upward by the mass of the air or liquid it displaces.

carbon cycle—The path carbon follows as it moves from the air to living tissue to the earth and back to the atmosphere. Carbon molecules may pass through the cycle quickly or, in the case of fossil fuels, it may take millions of years.

carbon dioxide—A greenhouse gas that is a key component in the process of photosynthesis. It is released by living cells during respiration.

chlorophyll—The green pigment in leaves that acts as a catalyst in the process of photosynthesis.

chord—A line connecting two points on the circumference of a circle.

decomposers—Bacteria and fungi that convert dead organic matter and waste into ammonia and other compounds.

denitrifying bacteria—Bacteria in soil that convert nitrates to nitrogen gas that enters the atmosphere.

desalination—A process by which salty ocean water can be converted to fresh water.

density—The ratio of mass to volume for any substance.

distillation—A method that uses heat to separate the components dissolved in a liquid.

global warming—The gradual warming of Earth due to an increase in greenhouse gases, such as carbon dioxide.

greenhouse gases—Atmospheric gases that reflect radiant heat energy back to Earth.

limewater—A solution of calcium hydroxide that is used to test for carbon dioxide. It turns milky when carbon dioxide is bubbled into it.

midday—A time midway between sunrise and sunset when the sun is highest in the sky and the shadows it casts are shortest.

nitrogen—A gaseous element that makes up 78 percent of Earth's atmosphere.

nitrogen cycle—The path that nitrogen follows as it moves from air to soil to living tissue and back to air.

nitrifying bacteria—Bacteria in soil that convert some nitrogen compounds to nitrate ions.

nitrogen-fixing bacteria—Bacteria that convert elemental atmospheric nitrogen to nitrogen compounds. They can be found on the roots of legume plants.

oxygen—A gas that makes up 21 percent of Earth's atmosphere. It enters cells during respiration and is essential to the "burning" of food to release energy.

oxygen cycle—The path that oxygen follows as it moves from air to living tissue and back to air.

perihelion—The point in the sun's orbit when it is closest to Earth (about 147 million kilometers, or 91 million miles).

phosphorus cycle—The path followed by phosphorus as it moves from soil to living tissue and back to soil or the ocean floor.

photosynthesis—A process in which green plants combine atmospheric carbon dioxide with water using energy from the sun to make food.

phototropism—The tendency of plants to turn toward light.

Polaris—The North Star, which lies almost directly above Earth's North Pole.

solar cycles—The sun's daily cycle (one rotation) and its annual cycle (one revolution about its orbit).

water cycle—The path that water follows as it moves from Earth to atmosphere and back.

Appendix: Science Supply Companies

Arbor Scientific
P.O. Box 2750
Ann Arbor, MI 48106-2750
(800) 367-6695
www.arborsci.com

Carolina Biological Supply Co.
2700 York Road
Burlington, NC 27215-3398
(800) 334-5551
http://www.carolina.com

Connecticut Valley Biological Supply Co., Inc.
82 Valley Road, Box 326
Southampton, MA 01073
(800) 628-7748
http://www.ctvalleybio.com

Delta Education
P.O. Box 3000
80 Northwest Blvd
Nashua, NH 03061-3000
(800) 258-1302
customerservice@delta-education.com

Edmund Scientific's Scientifics
60 Pearce Avenue
Tonawanda, NY 14150-6711
(800) 728-6999
http://www.scientificsonline.com

Educational Innovations, Inc.
362 Main Avenue
Norwalk, CT 06851
(888) 912-7474
http://www.teachersource.com

Fisher Science Education
4500 Turnberry
Hanover Park, IL 60133
(800) 955-1177
http://www.fisheredu.com

Frey Scientific
100 Paragon Parkway
Mansfield, OH 44903
(800) 225-3739
http://www.freyscientific.com

Nasco-Fort Atkinson
P.O. Box 901
Fort Atkinson, WI 53538-0901
(800) 558-9595
http:// www.enasco.com

Nasco-Modesto
P.O. Box 3837
Modesto, CA 95352-3837
(800) 558-9595
http://www.enasco.com

Sargent-Welch/VWR Scientific
P.O. Box 5229
Buffalo Grove, IL 60089-5229
(800) SAR-GENT
http://www.SargentWelch.com

Science Kit & Boreal Laboratories
777 East Park Drive
P.O. Box 5003
Tonawanda, NY 14150
(800) 828-7777
http://sciencekit.com

Wards Natural Science Establishment
P.O. Box 92912
Rochester, NY 14692-9012
(800) 962-2660
http://www.wardsci.com

Further Reading

Books

Bardhan-Quallen, Sudipta. ***Championship Science Fair Projects: 100 Sure-to-Win Experiments.*** New York: Sterling, 2005.

David, Sarah B. ***Reducing Your Carbon Footprint at Home.*** New York: The Rosen Publishing Group, Inc., 2009.

Jakob, Cheryl. ***The Water Cycle.*** North Mankato, Minn.: Smart Apple Media, 2008.

McKay, Kim and Jenny Bonnin. ***True Green Kids: 100 Things You Can Do to Save the Planet.*** Washington, D.C: National Geographic Society, 2008.

Rhadigan, Joe and Rain Newcomb. ***Prize-Winning Science Fair Projects for Curious Kids.*** New York: Lark Books, 2004.

Roston, Eric. ***The Carbon Age: How Life's Core Element Has Become Civilization's Greatest Threat.*** New York: Walker & Company, 2008.

Sobha, Geeta. ***Green Technology: Earth Friendly Innovations.*** New York: Crabtree Publishing Company, 2008.

Internet Addresses

The Carbon Cycle

<users.rcn.com/jkimball.ma.ultranet/BiologyPages/C/CarbonCycle.html>

The Nitrogen Cycle

<www.visionlearning.com/library/module_viewer.php?mid=98>

Index

A
acid rain, 42
air density, 63
algae, 85–86, 94
Alpha Centauri, 13
ammonium nitrite decomposition, 89
aphelion, 33
aquifers, 77–78
Archimedes, 62, 67
Austin, Thomas, 100
Australian rabbits, 99, 100

B
baking soda (sodium bicarbonate), 57, 64
Big Dipper, 19–21
birth rate, 95
buoyancy, 67

C
calcium carbonate, 56
carbon cycle
    decomposition, 43–44, 83–84
    global warming in, 40–42
    overview, 5, 37–40
carbon dioxide
    atmospheric, 41
    benefits of, 37, 55
    chemical test for, 56
    density, 63–67
    in exhaled air, 59–61
    photosynthesis and, 48–51
    properties of, 57–58
    reduction of, 25, 105
    sources of, 5, 39–42, 57
carnivores, 53
carrying capacity, 96, 104
celestial sphere, 26
chlorophyll extraction, 47
citric acid, 64
coal, 40
comets, 69
compasses, 21
conservation, 78–80, 104–106
corn, 86–87

D
death rate, 95
decomposition, 43–44, 83–84
deforestation, 41
desalination, 76
detergents, 79, 94
direction finding, 14–18
distillation, 73–75
doubling time, 96
drip irrigation, 78
Dubhe, 19, 20

E
Earth
    atmosphere composition, 40
    magnetic poles, 21
    orbit, 33
    water volume, 70
energy conservation, 105–106
equinoxes, 30, 33
escape velocity, 69–70
evaporation rates, 81–82
experiments, designing, 7–9

F
fertility rate, 95
fertilizers, 80, 84–85, 94
food shortages, 104
food storage in leaves, 46–47
fossil fuels, 5, 25, 39–42, 86

G
gas density measurement, 62–67
global warming, 25, 40–42, 55, 105
glucose, 39
greenhouse gases, 5, 40–42, 86
green tips, 78–80, 86, 105–106

H
hazardous wastes, 79, 80
heath hens, 100
helium density, 63
herbivores, 53
hydrocarbons, 39–40
hydrogen density, 63

I
irrigation, 76–78

L
leaves, food storage in, 46–47
light speed, 13
limewater (calcium hydroxide), 56
Little Dipper, 20, 21

M
Merak, 19, 20
methane, 40
midday time calculation, 15

N
nitrogen cycle, 83–86
nitrogen density, 63
nitrogen-fixing bacteria, 83
nitrogen gas isolation, 88–93
nitrous oxide, 86
north-south line checking, 19–21

O
ocean acidification, 42
ocean water evaporation, 73–75
octane, 40
Ogallala Aquifer, 77
omnivores, 53
organic farming, 86–87, 94
oxygen
  boiling point, 88
  content, removing, 85–86
  cycle, 37–40, 54
  density, 63
  percentage in air, 91

P
perihelion, 33
pH, 42
phosphates, 94
phosphorus cycle, 94
photosynthesis
  carbon dioxide and, 48–51
  food storage in leaves, 46–47
  light and, 52–54
  organic farming, 86
  overview, 37–38
  starch identification, 45
phototropism, 54
photovoltaic cells, 25
plants, adaptation in, 53–54
Polaris (North Star), 19–21
population cycles
  Australian rabbits, 99, 100
  human, 101–104
  modeling, 97–98
  overview, 95–96
population growth rate, 95

R
replacement rate, 96
respiration, 38–39, 54
rivers, 77–78

S
safety, 9–11
science fairs, 9–10
scientific method, 7–9
seasons, 22–24, 34–36
seltzer tablets, 64
soil conservation, 104–106
solar cycle
  daily, annual modeling, 29–31
  direction finding, 14–18
  north-south line checking, 19–21
  overview, 13
  seasons, 22–24, 34–36
  sunrise, sunset measurement, 22–24
  sun's path, mapping, 26–28
solar energy, 25
sphere volume calculation, 66
starch identification, 45
sunrise, sunset measurement, 22–24
sun's path, mapping, 26–28

T
toilets, 78–79
tropic of Capricorn, 35–36

V
variables, 7–8

W
water
  conservation of, 78–80
  evaporation, 73–75
  height ratio calculation, 91
  shortages, 76–78
water cycle
  modeling, 71–72
  ocean water evaporation, 73–75
  overview, 68–70